SKYSCRAPERS

INVESTIGATE FEATS OF ENGINEERING

Donna Latham

Illustrated by Andrew Christensen

~ Latest titles in the *Build It Yourself* Series ~

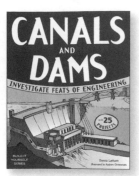
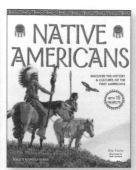
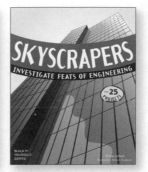

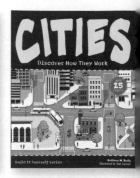

Check out more titles at www.nomadpress.net

Nomad Press
A division of Nomad Communications
10 9 8 7 6 5 4 3 2 1

This book was manufactured by Sheridan Books, Ann Arbor, MI USA.
September 2013, Job #349813
ISBN: 978-1-61930-189-4

Illustrations by Andrew Christensen
Educational Consultant, Marla Conn

Questions regarding the ordering of this book should be addressed to
Nomad Press
2456 Christian St.
White River Junction, VT 05001
www.nomadpress.net

Nomad Press is committed to preserving ancient forests and natural resources. We elected to print *Skyscrapers: Investigate Feats of Engineering* on Thor PCW containing 30% post consumer waste.

Nomad Press made this paper choice because our printer, Sheridan Books, is a member of Green Press Initiative, a nonprofit program dedicated to supporting authors, publishers, and suppliers in their efforts to reduce their use of fiber obtained from endangered forests.

For more information, visit **www.greenpressinitiative.org**.

CONTENTS

Glossary ❖ **Resources** ❖ **Index**

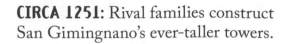

3000 BCE–500 BCE: The Babylonians, Sumerians, and Assyrians construct mammoth, pyramid-shaped towers, called ziggurats.

2600s BCE: Imhotep, the world's first named architect, lives and works in Egypt.

2650 BCE: The Egyptians first build pyramids, which rise from rectangular bases.

2600 BCE: Construction of Egypt's Bent Pyramid begins.

2000 BCE: The Ziggurat of Ur, which still stands today, is erected in what is today Iraq.

CIRCA 1500 BCE–800 BCE: Bronze Age builders on Sardinia construct thousands of unusual circular towers, called *nuraghi*.

CIRCA 607 CE: Japan's earthquake-resistant Sai-in pagoda is erected.

1173: In Italy, construction begins on the Leaning Tower of Pisa. Before the third story is built, the tower begins to tilt.

CIRCA 1251: Rival families construct San Gimingnano's ever-taller towers.

1854: Elisha Graves Otis patents elevator safety brakes. His inventions make reliable passenger elevators and skyscrapers possible.

1871: The Great Chicago Fire destroys Chicago and launches the "Great Rebuilding."

1880: Werner Von Siemens develops the first electric elevator.

1881: Thomas Edison devises New York's first electrical power and distribution center, which advances the building of skyscrapers.

1885: William Le Baron Jenney, "Father of the American Skyscraper," builds Chicago's Home Insurance Building. He revolutionizes architecture and engineering with steel-frame construction.

1888: Theophilus Van Kannel patents the Storm-Door Structure. It evolves into the revolving door, which is the entry of skyscrapers.

1889: When the Eiffel Tower is complete, it's the world's tallest structure.

1895: Chicago's Reliance Building, one of the first equipped with electricity, opens.

1930: New York's glamorous Chrysler Building becomes the world's tallest building with a sneaky spire. The victory is short-lived.

1931: New York's Empire State Building becomes the world's tallest building and uplifts spirits during the Depression.

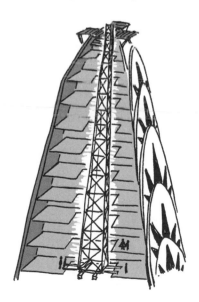

1972–1973: New York's World Trade Center Twin Towers become the world's tallest buildings.

1974: Chicago's Sears Tower (now called the Willis Tower), a bundled-tube construction, becomes the world's tallest building.

1989: San Francisco's seismic-resistant Transamerica Pyramid survives the magnitude 7.1 Loma Prieta earthquake.

1990: The Leaning Tower of Pisa closes for the first time in its history. It reopens in 2001, after soil engineer John Burland stabilizes the structure.

2001: Terrorist attacks demolish New York's World Trade Center Twin Towers.

2010: Chicago architect Jeanne Gang unveils Aqua, the world's tallest skyscraper created by a woman.

2010: Dubai's Burj Khalifa becomes the world's tallest building.

For Charles Mollenkamp,
builder of the future.

THE SKY'S THE LIMIT

DO YOU LIVE IN A CITY, OR HAVE YOU EVER VISITED A CITY?
What do you see towering in the **skyline**? At the place where
sky and land meet, a city's tall **structures** soar up into the
sky. Day and night, often visible from great distances, they form
a jagged manmade outline. **Skyscrapers**, towers, bridges,
and even Ferris wheels rise from the ground. Against the sky,
these **landmarks** create a city's skyline. No wonder people
call skylines a city's fingerprints! No two are the same.

WORDS to KNOW

skyline: an outline of land and buildings against the sky.

structure: something that is built, such as a building, bridge, tunnel, tower, or dam.

skyscraper: an extremely tall building.

landmark: an important structure or feature of the land that identifies a place and can be used to find or mark a location.

cityscape: a view of a city.

engineer: someone who uses science, math, and creativity to solve problems.

innovate: to come up with a new way of doing something.

technology: tools, methods, and systems used to solve a problem or do work.

Skyscrapers rule skylines in cities everywhere. Can you imagine Paris without the Eiffel Tower or New York City without the Empire State Building? Around the world, people take pride in their skylines. Seattle's Space Needle, Chicago's John Hancock Center, and Toronto's CN Tower are beloved landmarks. Anyone visiting these cities can quickly spot these magnificent structures in their **cityscapes**. It's hard to imagine these locations without them.

EARLY ENGINEERING

Engineers are people who use their imagination to **innovate** or design **technology** to help people, the environment, and all creatures on the planet. They use science and math, as well as experience, judgment, and common sense to turn an idea into a design that can be built by others. They come up with creative, useful solutions to improve our everyday lives—how we communicate, work, travel, stay healthy, and entertain ourselves.

TOWERING WITH HOPE FOR THE FUTURE

In 2001, devastating terrorist attacks blasted a hole through New York City's beloved skyline. The two World Trade Center towers **collapsed** after terrorists flew into the buildings with hijacked planes. The attacks killed nearly 3,000 people. Many people predicted the quest to build high into the sky would end, but it continues stronger than ever—both in the United States and around the world. In fact, about half of the world's skyscrapers have been built since 2000. Europe's tallest building is the Shard, in London. It reaches 1,016 feet high (310 meters) and was completed in 2012. Symbols of power, wealth, and progress, skyscrapers tower with hope for the future.

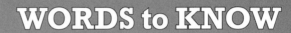

WORDS to KNOW

collapse: to fall in or down suddenly.

In 2011, on the 10th anniversary of the attack on the World Trade Center, a memorial courtyard opened with reflecting pools where the buildings once stood.

Did you know that **engineering** is as old as **civilization** itself?

It took thousands of years, and lots of **trial and error**, for engineers to figure out clever and creative ways to defy **gravity** in order to build big and build up.

Long ago, a tall structure started as just a spark of imagination. An early engineer chased an idea no one had thought of before. The earliest tall structures were built long before the study of **physics** and without modern technology, machines, and tools. Today, engineers and **architects** work together to make sure buildings are both safe and nice to look at.

WORDS to KNOW

engineering: the work done by engineers.

civilization: a community of people that is advanced in art, science, and government.

trial and error: trying first one thing, then another and another, until something works.

gravity: a physical force that draws everything toward the center of the earth.

physics: the science of how matter and energy work together.

architect: a person who designs buildings.

DID YOU KNOW?

The Eiffel Tower is one of the world's most identifiable structures. Many consider it an elegant work of art and a symbol of Paris. But when France built the crisscrossing iron structure for the World's Fair in 1889, not everyone liked the 1,050-foot-tall tower (320 meters). Some people complained that it was ugly. They called it the metal asparagus!

Cultures in **ancient Mesopotamia** started building tall structures as early as 3000 **BCE**. Until about 500 BCE, the people of this region constructed **ziggurats** using sun-dried mud-brick. Ziggurats were stepped pyramid-shaped towers that reached toward the sky, built to offer homes to the powerful gods believed to be living there. The tallest ziggurats were 200 feet high (61 meters). Some ziggurats, such as the Ziggurat of Ur, still survive in what is today Iraq and Iran.

Scholars believe ziggurats provided the model for the famous Egyptian pyramids.

WORDS to KNOW

culture: a group of people who share beliefs and a way of life.

ancient Mesopotamia: an area in what is today southern Iraq.

BCE: put after a date, BCE stands for Before Common Era and counts down to zero. CE stands for Common Era and counts up from zero. These non-religious terms correspond to BC and AD.

ziggurat: an ancient pyramid-shaped temple tower.

On the island of Sardinia in the Mediterranean Sea, there are nearly 7,000 circular towers called *nuraghi* built of rugged volcanic stone. No structures like them exist anywhere else in the world and most people don't even know about them! These marvels of engineering were built sometime between 3,000 and 4,000 years ago, around the same time the Egyptians built their pyramids.

THE LEANING TOWER OF PISA

The 184-foot-high Leaning Tower of Pisa (56 meters) is famous for its flaw! Construction on the white marble bell tower started in 1173. Before the third story was built, the tower started tilting. Over 800 years later, it's still standing—slanted. Why? The tower was built on squishy soil. The **foundation** was too weak to support the immense structure.

WORDS to KNOW

foundation: the part of a building below the ground that transfers and distributes the structure's weight.

From 1990 to 2001, officials closed the tower to the public for the first time in history because they feared it might fall over. John Burland, a professor of soil engineering, devised a plan to steady the tilting tower, and it has settled back into the ground. Today, tourists from around the world visit Pisa's amazing Leaning Tower. If you're like most people, if you ever visit the tower, you'll leave with a photo of yourself pretending to prop it up!

Notable Quotable

"Innovation . . . takes things we already know but synthesizes them in a totally new way."
—*Jeanne Gang (1964–), Chicago architect who designed the 82-story Aqua, the world's largest skyscraper designed by a woman.*

DID YOU KNOW?

Australia's stunning Sydney Opera House is the world's busiest performing arts center. This cherished symbol of the city's **waterscape** rises above Sydney Harbour. Its many white, **vaulted**, **geometric** "shells" are a modern wonder that gleam in sunlight and glow in moonlight.

TOWER OF JERICHO

The ancient Tower of Jericho, located near the city of Jerusalem, stands 28 feet tall (8½ meters) and is considered the world's first skyscraper. It took grueling work and cooperation to construct the tower. The tower was built inside the walls that protected the city. Some **archaeologists** believe it may have been a symbol of the power and unity existing

WORDS to KNOW

waterscape: a landscape with an expanse of water as a dominant feature.

vaulted: a building or room with an arched roof or roofs.

geometric: straight lines and simple shapes such as circles or squares.

archaeologist: someone who studies ancient cultures by looking at what they left behind.

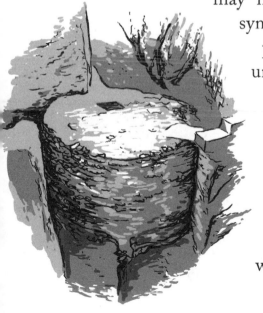

within the community. People built the monument with stone and supported it with plastered mud. A doorway at the bottom opened to an enclosed stairway. Steps led to the roof, where there may have been a lookout. Archaeologists estimate the tower is about 11,000 years old. At that time, it was probably Earth's tallest structure!

WORLD'S TALLEST ... FOR NOW

In 2010, Dubai's Burj Khalifa was crowned the world's tallest building. A building must have floors used as living or office space, otherwise it is classified as a tower. Sometimes a building has the word tower in its name, but don't let that confuse you. Burj Khalifa scrapes the sky at 2,717 feet (828 meters). Gleaming with glass and metal, Burj Khalifa remains the world's tallest building, structure, and freestanding tower. The top ten tallest buildings in the world in 2013 are:

1. **Burj Khalifa,** Dubai, 2,717 feet (828 meters), 2010

2. **Makkah Royal Clock Tower Hotel**, Mecca, Saudi Arabia, 1,972 feet (601 meters), 2012

3. **Taipei 101**, Taipei, Taiwan, 1,671 feet (509 meters), 2004

4. **Shanghai World Financial Center**, Shanghai, China, 1,614 feet (492 meters), 2008

5. **International Commerce Center**, Hong Kong, 1,588 feet (484 meters), 2010

6. and 7. **Petronas Twin Towers**, Kuala Lumpur, Malaysia, 1,483 feet (452 meters), 1998

8. **Zifeng Tower**, Nanjing, China, 1,476 feet (450 meters), 2010

9. **Willis Tower**, Chicago, Illinois, 1,454 feet (450 meters), 1974

10. **KK100**, Shenzhen, China, 1,449 feet (442 meters), 2011

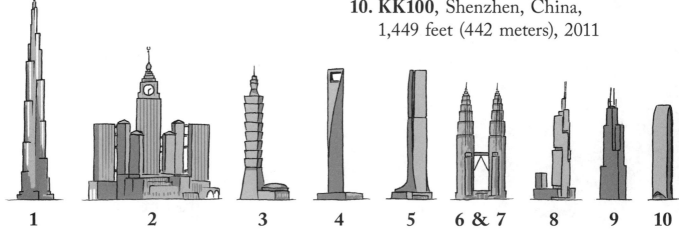

1   2   3   4   5   6 & 7   8   9   10

TALLEST STRUCTURE

Toronto's CN Tower is an observation and communications tower completed in 1976. It defines that city's skyline. At 1,815 feet (553 meters), the celebrated landmark was the world's tallest freestanding structure on land for over 30 years. It took 40 months for 1,537 workers working 24 hours a day, five days a week to complete the tower. Every year, over 1.5 million tourists ride its six elevators to reach the observation deck for spectacular views stretching over 100 miles (160 kilometers)—all the way to Niagara Falls on a clear day. You can eat at the top in its spinning restaurant!

ABOUT THE PROJECTS

Build the projects in this book to understand how skyscrapers are built. See what happens when they succeed and when they fail. Most of the projects in this book involve items you might have around the house. Remember that safety's first, so ask adults for help when handling raw eggs, sharp objects, and matches.

Use the activities to make your own discoveries about skyscrapers and other marvels of engineering. Along the way you'll engage in the engineering process. Let your ideas and ingenuity spark your own innovations.

ENGINEERING AND THINKING BIG

YOU PROBABLY DON'T REALIZE HOW FASCINATING THE engineering profession is. Every bridge we travel across, every train, bus, or bicycle we ride, every gadget we use was once just a dream in an engineer's imagination. From pizza slicers and smoothie blenders, hockey facemasks and snowboard ramps, to tablet apps and ultra-portable laptop computers, we have engineers to thank for their creation.

ENGINEERING AND THINKING BIG

Today we have phones and computers that communicate without wires, spacecraft to explore the universe, and animations where imaginary characters and creatures look real. Robots can operate on people, while doctors control the robot over the Internet from thousands of miles away!

This is all possible because of the men and women in engineering who work together to turn dreams into reality.

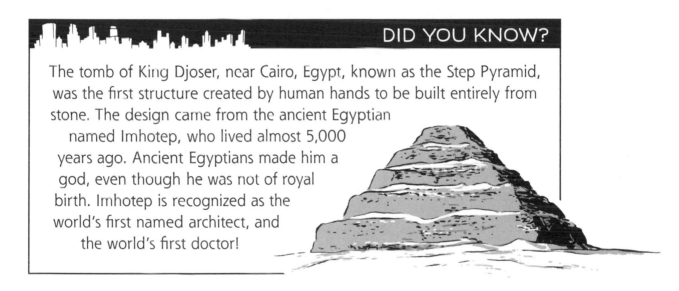

DID YOU KNOW?

The tomb of King Djoser, near Cairo, Egypt, known as the Step Pyramid, was the first structure created by human hands to be built entirely from stone. The design came from the ancient Egyptian named Imhotep, who lived almost 5,000 years ago. Ancient Egyptians made him a god, even though he was not of royal birth. Imhotep is recognized as the world's first named architect, and the world's first doctor!

BRANCHES OF ENGINEERING

There are many kinds of engineers. There are civil and environmental engineers, electrical and computer engineers, chemical, mechanical, and biomedical engineers. All engineers use math and science as building blocks for their designs, but the most important characteristic an engineer must possess is imagination.

Five Major Branches of Engineering	
CHEMICAL	Using science to convert raw materials and chemicals into things people can use, such as food and energy products.
CIVIL	Designing and building bridges, buildings, dams, highways, and tunnels.
COMPUTER	Designing technology such as computer software and hardware, wireless communication networks, touch screen tablets, and smartphone apps.
ELECTRICAL	Designing electrical systems and electronic products such as solar power systems, batteries for electric cars, and light bulbs that use very little electricity.
MECHANICAL	Designing mechanical systems such as engines, tools, machines, spaceships, and even robots.

CLIMBING HIGH IN CHICAGO

In 2012, as the crowd went wild, 31-year-old Zac Vawter made history. He was the first to climb the stairs 103 floors up Chicago's Willis Tower to its Sky Deck with a **bionic** leg! Vawter finished his historic climb in around 45 minutes, with no breaks.

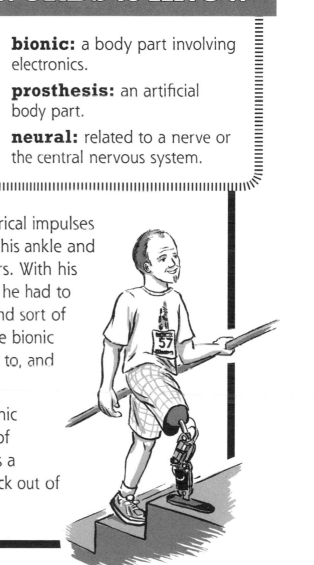

Several years earlier, Vawter lost his right leg after a motorcycle crash. Today, he uses his mind to control the multi-million-dollar, 10-pound motorized smart limb (4½ kilos). When Vawter thinks about climbing stairs, electronics, belts, chains, and motors whir into action. The robotic leg responds to electrical impulses from Vawter's hamstring muscles to move his ankle and knee. He is thrilled to be walking up stairs. With his standard **prosthesis**, he described that he had to "take every step with my good foot first and sort of lift or drag the prosthetic leg up. With the bionic leg, it's simple. I take the stairs like I used to, and can even take two at a time."

Neural engineers in the Center for Bionic Research at the Rehabilitation Institute of Chicago continue to perfect the limb. As a software engineer, Vawter gets an extra kick out of learning how the bionic leg operates.

WORDS to KNOW

bionic: a body part involving electronics.

prosthesis: an artificial body part.

neural: related to a nerve or the central nervous system.

CIVIL ENGINEERING

According to the US Department of Labor, Bureau of Statistics, engineers hold about 1.6 million jobs in the United States. **Civil engineering** is nicknamed the mother of all engineering disciplines because it is the oldest branch of engineering. Civil engineers design **public works** such as roads, bridges, dams, canals, ports, railways, and airports. Civil engineers think big to construct safe skyscrapers, applying scientific and mathematical knowledge to solve problems by asking questions. What are the most effective methods and materials to use? How can we build a skyscraper that won't collapse? How can it stand up to ferocious winds and withstand the horizontal and vertical shaking of earthquakes? What shape and which materials will make the skyscraper sturdy in the rock and soil below?

WORDS to KNOW

civil engineering: the branch of engineering that deals with the design, construction, and maintenance of public works and public buildings or spaces.

public work: a construction project such as a highway or dam that is paid for by the government for use by anyone.

ENGINEERING DESIGN PROCESS

Do you like to work with others? Engineering is a group effort that allows for the open exchange of ideas. Engineers apply knowledge gained from past successes and failures to new innovations and projects. The engineering design process is a series of steps engineers follow when they tackle a problem. The steps lead to a solution such as a new product, system, or structure.

1. **Identify the Problem:** In the first step, engineers figure out what they must accomplish. They pose questions to target their goal. They research and gather information.

2. **Brainstorm Solutions:** In a group, engineers share creative, sudden ideas no matter how impossible they may seem. One clever idea launches a domino effect of other solutions or methods. After brainstorming, engineers sort the ideas to target the most likely solution and focus on it.

3. **Design and Simulate:** Engineers draw a solution diagram. They note the tools and building materials required. Using computer programs, engineers are able to simulate their design to experiment with different variations before moving to the next step.

4. **Build a Prototype:** A **prototype** is an important component of testing and research. It allows engineers to notice things they may have overlooked. Others can share their ideas for improvement or see something that might not work.

WORDS to KNOW

prototype: a working model or mock-up that allows engineers to test their solution.

5. **Test the Prototype:** As a team, engineers conduct tests. They observe how the prototype measures up to the design.

6. **Evaluate Success:** Engineers discuss what worked and what didn't work with the design. They share ideas for improvements in design or materials.

7. **Redesign with Improvements:** Engineers apply suggestions for improvement and develop a stronger product to simulate and test.

ENGINEERING DESIGN PROCESS

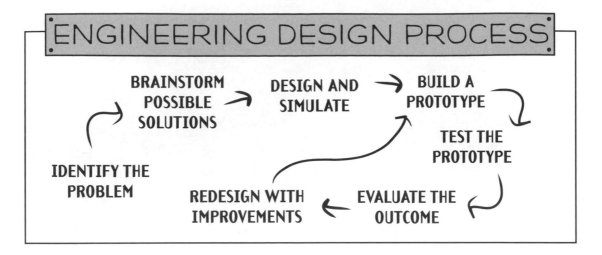

BRAINSTORM POSSIBLE SOLUTIONS → DESIGN AND SIMULATE → BUILD A PROTOTYPE → TEST THE PROTOTYPE

IDENTIFY THE PROBLEM

REDESIGN WITH IMPROVEMENTS ← EVALUATE THE OUTCOME

Do you notice how the engineering design process flow chart connects the steps with arrows? That keeps the design process **open-ended**. Engineers might have to throw out one idea and come up with a new solution. They might double back to revisit a step or two. An earlier idea that was rejected might turn out to be promising. Frequently, several solutions are possible, so engineers devise multiple prototypes.

WORDS to KNOW

open-ended: able to adapt to the needs of a situation.

matter: what an object is made of.

energy: the ability to do work.

force: a push or pull that changes an object's motion.

FORCES: PUSHES AND PULLS

Physics is a branch of science that deals with the physical world. It centers on **matter** and **energy** and their interactions. Engineers apply principals of physics to build structures that resist **forces**. A force is a push or pull. Forces make things move or change position.

The forces that are exerted on big structures like skyscrapers are called **loads**. What happens if a structure can't withstand wind pressure? It splits apart and collapses. Skyscrapers must be **structurally sound**. They must be **stable**.

PUSH

PULL

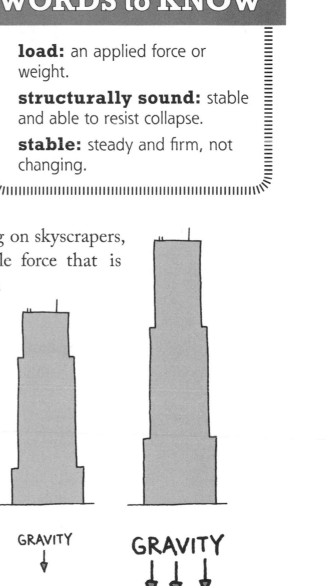

WORDS to KNOW

load: an applied force or weight.

structurally sound: stable and able to resist collapse.

stable: steady and firm, not changing.

What is one force that is always pulling on skyscrapers, and on you? Gravity. This is an invisible force that is acting on you right now. Even though you can't feel it, gravity is constantly pulling you and everything on the earth toward the earth's center. It holds you on the ground so you don't float like an astronaut in space.

To stand vertically, lofty buildings must withstand gravity's natural force. The higher a structure stands, the greater gravity's downward force pushes on it. Proper support is essential to keep vertical structures like skyscrapers standing.

GRAVITY

GRAVITY

WORDS to KNOW

tension: a pulling force that pulls or stretches a material outward.

compression: a pushing force that squeezes or presses a material inward.

snapping: the splitting apart that occurs when the force of tension overcomes an object's ability to handle that tension.

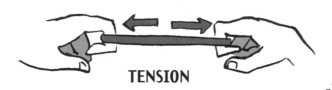

TENSION

PULLING TENSION AND PUSHING COMPRESSION

To build tall, engineers balance **tension** and **compression**. These are the primary forces that keep structures standing—or cause them to tumble down. Tension is a pulling force that tugs an object or material outward. Tension stretches objects, yanking them so much they usually grow longer. Objects can even break or split.

What happens when you stretch a rubber band? It lengthens because it's under tension. When steel cables hoist a jam-packed elevator to a skyscraper's top floor, the cables are in tension. **Snapping** occurs when tension's force overcomes an object's ability to handle that tension. If you pull a rubber band with excessive force, what happens? It snaps apart.

Compression is a pushing force. It pushes an object or material inward. Compression squishes objects together. It usually causes them to shorten. As they support their own enormous

COMPRESSION

weight, skyscrapers experience compression. When you squeeze a foam ball, it compresses. It gets shorter and smaller.

What happens when compression's force overcomes an object's capacity to handle that compression? **Buckling** occurs. When you squash an empty beverage can, you are compressing it to the point that it buckles. If building materials buckle, then a structure is in danger of collapse. When a blizzard dumps snow and ice on a garage roof, the roof can buckle, caving in under pressure.

TWISTING TORSION AND SLIDING SHEAR

Torsion is a twisting force. When you wring out a wet sponge, you apply torsion. High winds can cause broadcast towers to twist so violently they fall down.

Shear is a sliding force. When shear is applied to an object, parts of it move past one another. The force goes in different directions. When you use scissors to cut a piece of string, you use shear force. The handles move in opposite directions, placing force on the screw that connects them so the blades slide and cut the string. When an earthquake jolts a skyscraper's support column, parts of the column can slip against one another causing the column to tumble down and the skyscraper to collapse.

WORDS to KNOW

buckling: the sudden crumbling or falling down that occurs when the force of compression overcomes an object's capacity to handle that compression.

torsion: a twisting force that turns or twirls a material.

shear: a sliding force that slips parts of a material in opposite directions.

TORSION

SHEAR

TRY THIS

Test compression and tension forces! Use a marshmallow, licorice stick, and piece of dry spaghetti. Place force on the marshmallow, compressing it by pressing on the top. Notice how it squishes and shortens. Does it hold up under pressure? Now apply tension by pulling the sides. What happens?

Vertically stand the licorice. Compress it lightly by pushing down on the top with one finger. Does the licorice hold up against the force? What if you push harder? Now hold the top with one finger. Push the side with another. Does the licorice bend sideways and buckle? To demonstrate tension, pull the ends of the licorice in opposite directions. How much force does it take to pull it apart?

Horizontally hold the spaghetti. With your index fingers, push on either end until the spaghetti bends sideways. Keep pushing. As tension builds up inside, it becomes strong enough to snap the spaghetti. Why don't the marshmallow and licorice easily snap? They are made of flexible materials. Brittle spaghetti is likely to splinter.

LOADS OF LOADS

To build structures, engineers use **statics**. This area of physics addresses forces and ways they produce **equilibrium**. To stay static, structures must withstand forces and loads. First engineers consider a structure's own weight, which is its **dead load**.

WORDS to KNOW

statics: how forces work together to keep objects in balance.

equilibrium: the state of balance between opposing forces.

dead load: the actual, constant weight of a structure.

A skyscraper's dead load is huge.

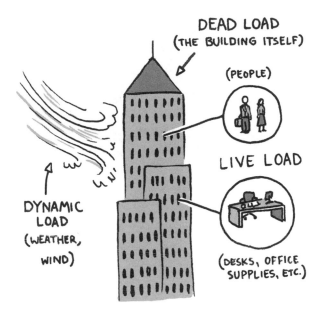

DEAD LOAD
(THE BUILDING ITSELF)

(PEOPLE)

LIVE LOAD

DYNAMIC
LOAD
(WEATHER,
WIND)

(DESKS, OFFICE
SUPPLIES, ETC.)

WORDS to KNOW

facade: the outside or front of a building.

live load: the changing weight of vehicles, people, furniture, and other things that are placed on a structure.

dynamic load: load that changes over time and is applied through motion.

tremor: a shaking movement or small earthquake.

The dead load consists of a jumbo base and concrete-embedded steel columns. It includes concrete floors, stone **facades**, and glass windows. Engineers must also consider **live loads**. These are people and objects acting on a structure. What's included in a skyscraper's live load? Elevators filled with people and offices crammed with desks, chairs, and computers. Observation decks teeming with tourists contribute, too. Live loads don't always stay the same.

Dynamic loads applied to structures through motion change too, which makes them unpredictable. Gale-force winds, swirling floodwaters, and Earth's **tremors** affect structures of all sizes.

DID YOU KNOW?

Rocks experience tension and compression. These pushing and pulling forces sometimes become too much for rocks, causing them to break and shift. As rock masses move, the result can be an earthquake as the rocks lurch into place.

Skyscrapers must resist environmental forces like hurricanes and violent earthquakes. While collapse is sometimes a reality, most buildings stay standing through all of these forces. We have engineers to thank for doing such a good job designing them.

DID YOU KNOW?

Structurally, spires are considered parts of a skyscraper, while antennae are not. People have clashed over which should be counted toward the height of a building. The Council on Tall Buildings and Urban Habitats has devised official criteria for skyscraper height measurement, which measures height to a building's tip—no matter what tops it!

SIR ISAAC NEWTON

Sir Isaac Newton was an English physicist and mathematician who lived from 1642 to 1727. He invented three laws of motion to explain gravity and other forces.

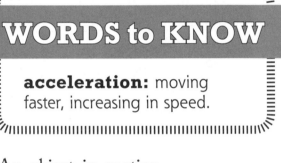

WORDS to KNOW

acceleration: moving faster, increasing in speed.

- **Newton's first law of motion:** An object at rest remains at rest unless acted on by a force. An object in motion continues in motion with the same speed and in the same direction unless acted upon by a force.

- **Newton's second law of motion: Acceleration** is produced when a force acts on a mass. The greater the mass of the object being accelerated, the greater the amount of force needed to accelerate the object.

- **Newton's third law of motion:** For every action there is an equal and opposite reaction.

SKYSCRAPER PENDULUMS

Before the 1880s, people used the word *skyscraper* to describe a ship with a tall mast. That's fitting because skyscrapers can cause motion sickness that feels just like seasickness! When high winds make tall buildings sway back and forth, people can feel sick from the motion.

When a wind gust slams you backward, do you shift your weight, bending in the opposite direction into the wind? Skyscrapers do something similar. Chicago's Park Tower, completed in 2000, is a sleek 70-story skyscraper. It was the United States' first building originally designed with a tuned mass damper (TMD). The TMD is a gigantic **pendulum** that relies on Newton's second law of motion. This law states that when a force acts on a mass, acceleration occurs. The larger the object's mass, the greater the force required to make it accelerate.

The TMD, rather than the skyscraper itself, absorbs the wind's motion and limits the wind's effect. If the skyscraper sways in one direction, the 300-ton TMD's colossal mass counteracts the wind's swinging stress by sliding in the opposite direction to stabilize the building. It keeps the structure at rest. The Park Tower doesn't wobble and make everyone inside woozy!

WORDS to KNOW

pendulum: a weight hung from a fixed support so it swings by gravity.

DID YOU KNOW?

Dizzying amusement park rides swing with pendulums! Busch Garden's gravity-defying Battering Ram rocks screaming riders to thrilling heights. King's Dominion SkyFlyer combines hang-gliding and skydiving.

Hit the Wall!

Supplies: *science journal and pencil, 3 hardcover books of equal size, heavy piece of cardboard, yardstick or measuring tape, 1 thick hardcover book (such as a dictionary), large washer, medium-sized toy car*

In this experiment with **inertia**, build a ramp and test a toy car to determine how it responds when it hits a wall. How will the ramp's height impact the distance traveled?

WORDS to KNOW

inertia: the tendency of a body at rest to remain at rest or a body in motion to stay in motion—until a force acts on it.

| Identify the problem you are trying to solve. What are some questions you can ask about it? Make your predictions about what will happen in your science journal. Make a data chart like the one shown.

2 Build the ramp on a flat surface by stacking the smaller books. Slant the cardboard against the books to form a ramp. Position one end so it rises about 4 inches (10 centimeters) above the top of the stack. Measure the ramp's height and length and note it on the data chart.

3 With the thick book, make a wall at the bottom of the ramp, opposite the stack.

DID YOU KNOW?

Newton's first law of motion is also called the Law of Inertia.

4 Position the washer on top of the car. You may need to hold the washer in place while you place the car at the ramp's top. Gently release the car without pushing it. Allow it to hit the wall made by your hardcover book.

5 Leave the car in place while you measure how far the washer launched. Record it on the data chart under Trial 1 Distance.

6 Repeat steps 4 and 5 as you conduct two more distance trials. Jot down the washer's travel distances.

7 Alter the height and length of the ramp and try the experiment again a few times.

8 Assess your data. What conclusions can you draw about the ramp's height and the distance the washer launched? What role did inertia play in the experiment?

Ramp Height & Length	Trial 1 Distance		Trial 2 Distance		Trial 3 Distance	
	Predicted	Actual	Predicted	Actual	Predicted	Actual

Oscillation Fascination

Supplies: *paper clip, 4 feet of string (1+ meter), science journal and pencil, table or doorway, tape, measuring tape, washer, stopwatch, scissors*

The Park Tower's TMD is an enormous pendulum. When a pendulum oscillates, it swings first one way, and then the other way. An oscillation is one back-and-forth movement. The length of time it takes for one oscillation to occur is called a period. When you construct a simple pendulum, how will the length of the string impact its period of oscillation?

1 Build the pendulum by tightly tying the paper clip to one end of the string. Predict how string length will affect a period. Create a data chart in your science journal.

2 Allow the clip to dangle from the string. Before you tape the string's opposite end to a table or countertop or in a doorway, measure the string length. You want your paper clip pendulum to swing from exactly 40 inches of string (102 centimeters).

3 Tape the string in place, remeasure, and, if necessary, adjust and re-tape the string. Make sure the clip can swing freely.

DID YOU KNOW?

Tightrope walkers often balance with parasols, poles, and hoops. But some tightrope walkers go freestyle, using only their bodies to help them balance. With their arms extended perpendicular to their torsos, freestyle walkers increase inertia by walking slowly. What happens when freestylers sway? They're like an oscillator with a long period. That period allows walkers a longer time to correct a wobbly movement, so they don't tumble off the wire.

4 Hook the washer onto the paperclip so it hangs from the paperclip.

5 You're ready to test pendulum periods! Hold the stopwatch in one hand. Grasp the washer with the other. At an angle, pull the washer to one side. Release the washer. Start the stopwatch. Count the number of oscillations that occur in 30 seconds.

6 Conduct three trials at about the same angle. Note the number of oscillations for each and record the data on your chart. Average the number and record this on the chart.

7 Repeat the experiment with three more lengths of string, each time 4 inches shorter than the one before (10 centimeters shorter), until you completely fill in the chart.

8 Assess your data. As string length decreased, did the speed of the period increase or decrease? How accurate was your prediction? What conclusions do you draw?

String Length	Trial 1 Number of Oscillations	Trial 2 Number of Oscillations	Trial 3 Number of Oscillations
40 inches (101 centimeters)			
36 inches (91 centimeters)			
32 inches (81 centimeters)			
28 inches (71 centimeters)			

A-Maze-ing Marble Motion

Supplies: *scissors, black construction paper, shoebox lid, glue, white construction paper, pencil, scratch paper, ruler, plastic drinking straws, marble*

Design a marble maze to illustrate Newton's first law of motion!

1 Cut the black paper to fit inside the shoebox lid. Glue the paper inside the lid to make the maze's background.

2 On the white paper, draw the outline of a skyscraper with a spire. Cut out the skyscraper shape and glue it to the background.

3 On scratch paper, design the maze within the outline of the skyscraper. Include unobstructed runways where the marble will freely move and dead ends to trap the marble. Experiment with different shapes and directions. How about a zigzag runway? A y-shaped one? Include a "Begin" area at the skyscraper's bottom center. How can you arrange straws to allow the marble to leave the "Begin" area? Add an "End" area at the top of the spire. How will your design trap the marble in place at the spire?

4 Draw your maze on the white skyscraper in the shoebox lid, then build it using the ruler, straws, scissors, and glue. Allow the glue to dry thoroughly.

5 To demonstrate inertia, place the marble in the "Begin" space. Hold the shoebox lid to keep the marble at rest. Predict how you can apply force to send it into motion. Test your prediction to get the marble rolling. Predict what will happen when the marble meets an obstruction. How does it illustrate Newton's first law of motion?

Egg Inertia

Supplies: *3 wide-mouth plastic cups, water, metal pizza pan, 3 cardboard tubes, 3 hard-boiled eggs, broom*

An object stays at rest until a force acts on it. Can you make eggs fly off their perches and into cups of water? Observe Newton's first law of motion with a famous science trick!

1 Set up the experiment by filling the cups with water and placing them on a steady surface. Place the pizza pan over the cups. Position the tubes on the pan over the center of each cup and place one egg on each tube.

2 Here's the tricky part! You need to transfer energy to the eggs so they launch off the tubes. With the broom handle, carefully whack the pan's side. This applies force to the eggs, which are at rest. Does the pan fly away? What happens to the eggs? Downward inertia should send them into the cups.

3 If the pan didn't launch off, then try, try, again. Figure out a different way to rap it. Will it work better to hit the pan with the broom at an angle? By swinging it like a bat?

TRY THIS

Experiment with one hard-boiled and one raw. Place them on their sides on a smooth surface. Predict what will happen when you spin them. Spin the hard-boiled egg first. Stop it with your fingertip, then release your finger. What happens? Now, spin the raw egg, stop it with your finger, and release it. Do the eggs respond differently? Why? What's different about the eggs that could explain the results?

DEFYING GRAVITY

SKYSCRAPERS ARE VERTICAL STRUCTURES THAT MUST REMAIN UPRIGHT.
Why don't they tip over? Why don't they sink straight into the ground,
or crumble and fall apart? The natural forces of gravity and wind push
against skyscrapers. In parts of the world where there are earthquakes,
seismic activity can shake the ground on which skyscrapers stand.
Yet skyscrapers stretching hundreds and hundreds of feet into the air
can still bear their own dead loads and support the live loads of the
people who live and work in there. They can do this because engineers
consider a balance of forces—gravity, tension, and compression.

BELOW AND ABOVE GROUND

As engineers build up, gravity's force pushes down. What keeps a tall building from keeling over? Its **center of gravity** is the point where gravity is concentrated.

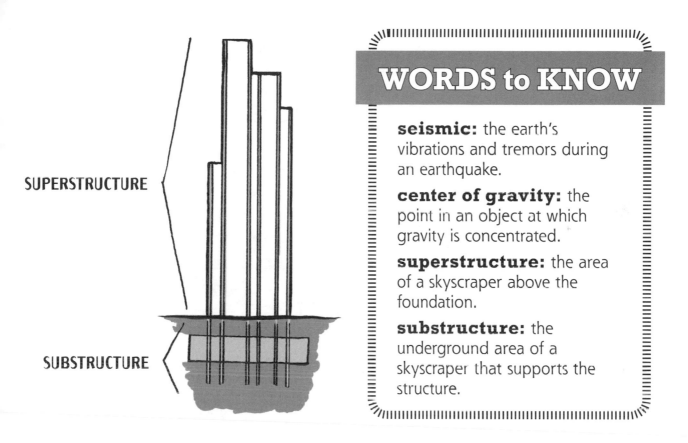

SUPERSTRUCTURE

SUBSTRUCTURE

WORDS to KNOW

seismic: the earth's vibrations and tremors during an earthquake.

center of gravity: the point in an object at which gravity is concentrated.

superstructure: the area of a skyscraper above the foundation.

substructure: the underground area of a skyscraper that supports the structure.

When you peer up from the ground, a long, thin **superstructure** appears top-heavy, with its massive weight concentrated at the top. To keep a skyscraper stable, engineers design it with a center of gravity underground in the **substructure**.

What you don't see is a hidden feat of engineering!

31

WORDS to KNOW

excavate: to dig out material from the ground.

bedrock: the layer of solid rock deep underground, under the top layer of soil and loose rock.

footing: an embedded anchor for columns in a foundation.

column: a vertical support structure.

skeleton frame: a skyscraper's support structure.

Workers **excavate** the soil, which is too weak for skyscrapers to stand on. They blast down to the sturdy **bedrock** to construct a deep, wide foundation that gives the building a low center of gravity. This critical underground base transfers and distributes the structure's weight. **Footings** drilled into solid rock provide the foundation for support **columns**. Wider than the tower itself, the foundation anchors and supports the soaring structure.

COMPRESSION AND TENSION IN STEELY SUPERSTRUCTURES

To balance the forces of gravity, nature, and loads, engineers consider the pulling force of tension and the pushing force of compression in building materials and in design. They use materials strong in both tension and compression, such as steel, which is made of iron combined with carbon, chromium, manganese, and nickel.

The superstructure is the building's bones and skin.

Just as your skeleton provides your body's framework, a steel **skeleton frame** forms a skyscraper's support structure.

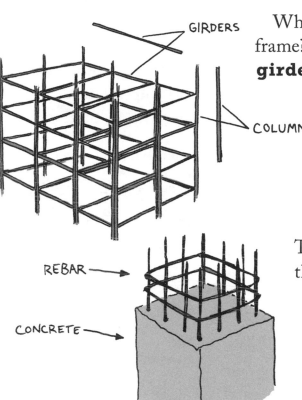

GIRDERS

COLUMNS

REBAR

CONCRETE

What are the parts of this skeleton frame? A building's huge weight rests on **girders**. These strong steel beams are typically straight and horizontal. Under a load, a girder's center flexes downward. Bending places the beam's top in compression. It places the bottom under tension.

Columns are straight and vertical. They support the girders, which places the columns under compression. Force moves along the columns and is sent down into the foundation.

WORDS to KNOW

girder: a strong horizontal supporting beam, usually made of steel.

rebar: a reinforced steel bar that is added to concrete to make a stronger building material.

Columns are made with concrete poured around **rebar**. Concrete is strong under compression, but it can become brittle and crack, so it's weak in tension. Rebar adds strength to the concrete so it can withstand tension loads. When rebar is set inside concrete, it forms a combined building material called reinforced concrete. Under the pulling force of tension and the sliding force of shear, reinforced concrete doesn't fracture and break apart as easily as regular concrete. This is especially important in areas that have earthquakes.

After constructing a skyscraper's bones, the skin goes on. **Curtain walls** protect the interior of the building from the forces of wind and weather. With a strong steel skeleton, curtain walls don't need to support any weight other than their own. Many modern skyscrapers feature glass walls that drench buildings with natural light and allow for breathtaking views from the inside.

EQUAL AND OPPOSITE

How do engineers apply concepts of physical science to build skyscrapers? They use Newton's third law of motion, which states, "For every action (force) there is an equal and opposite reaction (force)." When you prepare to push a heavy object, do you anchor and support yourself? Perhaps you bend your knees, drop your head, and lean forward. You're **braced** for the object's heavy weight to push you back, sending you in the opposite direction. What happens when wind's force pushes a skyscraper? Underground, the foundation shoves back.

WORDS to KNOW

curtain walls: the outside skin of a skyscraper, often made of windows.

brace: to support or strengthen.

thrust: a reactive pressure or force.

DID YOU KNOW?

You can use a balloon to demonstrate action-reaction **thrust**. Fully blow up a balloon. Pinch the open end tightly to keep air inside. Then release the end and observe what happens as air escapes. When air's force pours from the balloon in one direction, does it launch the balloon in the opposite direction?

BLOWING IN THE WIND

Wind engineering is a critical component of skyscraper design. Wind is moving air that puts **wind load** on a structure. Skyscrapers must absorb the stress from wind's enormous load. When wind's force smacks one side of a building, the columns respond. On the side where the wind hits, the columns stretch apart vertically. At the opposite side, away from the source of the wind, the columns squash together.

WORDS to KNOW

wind load: the force of moving air on a structure.

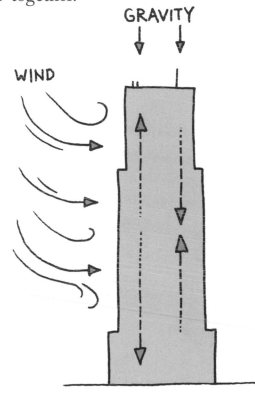

A skyscraper's columns and girders make a rigid spine that can hold up to wind's force. Some buildings use cross bracing, or X-bracing, on the exterior to stiffen the structure. Under the force of the wind, the braces squeeze together.

Look at a picture of the John Hancock Center in Chicago and find the Xs!

Notable Quotable

"If we all did the things we are capable of, we would astound ourselves."
—*Thomas Edison (1847–1931), inventor of the electric light*

TRANSAMERICA PYRAMID

In 1989, when a magnitude 7.1 earthquake rattled California's Santa Cruz Mountains, powerful seismic forces rocked San Francisco 60 miles from the epicenter (97 kilometers). The most severe earthquake to hit the city since 1906 killed more than 60 people, injured nearly 4,000, and left nearly 12,000 homeless. Tremors collapsed a top deck of the Oakland Bay Bridge. Buildings crumbled into rubble. In all, the catastrophic quake caused over $6 billion in property damage.

In San Francisco's financial district, terrified occupants of the city's tallest skyscraper braced themselves as it swayed for more than a minute. No one was injured. The 853-foot (260-meter) Transamerica Pyramid stood undamaged, an earthquake-proof feat of engineering.

WORDS to KNOW

truss: a network of beams and bars that rely on triangles to support a load.

Seismic forces shake structures horizontally and vertically. Earthquake engineers design structures and systems to withstand earthquakes and reduce seismic damage. They build earthquake-resistant structures like the magnificent winged Transamerica Pyramid, with its immense 52-foot-deep foundation (16 meters). A **truss** system with X-bracing above the first floor supports horizontal and vertical loads at the base. On each floor, reinforcing rods brace the building in four different places. The system withstands torsional forces during seismic events.

TRUSS SYSTEM

Build an Anemometer

Supplies: *egg carton, scissors, markers, 2 long straws, clear tape, pushpin, sharp pencil with an eraser, stopwatch*

The higher up a skyscraper soars, the more wind speed it must withstand. An anemometer is an instrument that measures the speed of the wind. Construct your own anemometer to measure approximate wind speed.

1 Cut out four separate egg cups from the carton. Make a design with the markers on one cup and set the cups to one side.

2 Make an X with the straws and tape the center of the X securely with clear tape.

3 Tape one egg cup to the end of each straw so they all face the same direction.

4 Push the pin through the straw X and into the eraser end of the pencil. The X needs to spin freely.

5 Take your anemometer outside on a windy day. Push the sharp end of the pencil into the ground.

6 The egg cup with the design is your starting point. Using a stopwatch, count how many times it goes by in one minute. This number tells you the speed of the wind. For example, two revolutions per minute could mean that the wind speed is 2 miles per hour (3 kilometers). Try your anemometer in different locations on the same day to see what might affect wind speed.

Center of Gravity Challenge

Supplies: *sturdy chair with an upright back, science journal and pencil, wall, dollar bill*

What do inching across a tightrope, pedaling a bike, and wakeboarding have in common? All rely on center of gravity for stability, mobility, and balance. Your center of gravity is probably located near your belly. But it shifts and changes with movement. Explore yours as you test yourself.

1 Sit in the chair. Now stand up. How much effort did it take? Was it easy? Now stand and hop forward on both legs. Was that easy for you?

2 Balance on one foot. What do you need to do to remain balanced? Do you need to shift your weight?

3 Copy the data chart from the next page and complete the First Trial areas for each activity tested. What conclusions can you draw about these movements?

4 For the Second Trial, complete the same actions with adjustments. Sit in the chair with your feet flat on the floor in front of you. Dangle your arms at your sides. Can you stand without using your hands and without leaning forward? To stand, you need to shift your center of gravity from over the chair to over your feet. With a no-leaning restriction, standing is impossible for many people.

Notable Quotable

"Life is like riding a bicycle. In order to keep your balance, you must keep moving."
—*Albert Einstein (1879–1955), physicist and winner of the Nobel Prize*

5 Can you hop while holding your toes? With both feet together, reach for your toes. Bend your knees if necessary so you can grasp your toes with both hands. Can you hop? Can you shift your center of gravity over your feet when you're clutching your toes?

6 What will happen when you balance with one arm and one foot against a wall? Stand sideways at the wall with your right arm and right foot against it. Can you lift your left leg? This is an extremely difficult movement. To balance on your right foot, your center of gravity must be over your right foot. The wall prevents you from leaning. Most people can't balance.

7 Complete the data chart with your Second Trial results. Assess your findings. What conclusions can you draw about center of gravity?

Stand	Hop	Balance
First Trial:	First Trial:	First Trial:
Second Trial:	Second Trial:	Second Trial:

TRY THIS

Stand with your back and heels against a wall and feet together. Have someone place a dollar bill on the floor 12 inches (30 centimeters) in front of you. Can you pick it up without bending your knees or shifting your feet? It's impossible! Why? As you stand against the wall, your center of gravity is over your feet. When you bend, the wall prevents your center of gravity from shifting. Since you can't move your feet, you lose your balance. Try the same thing away from the wall to see how your body shifts its weight.

39

Clown Around With Center of Gravity

Supplies: *clown pattern (online at nomadpress.net/templates), scissors, pencil with eraser, file folder, colored markers, tape, 2 pennies, 2 chairs with upright backs, string*

Use trial and error to create a balancing clown. Will it balance on a tightrope?

1 Go to **nomadpress.net/templates** and print the clown pattern template. Cut out the template and trace it onto the file folder. After you decorate your clown with markers, cut it out.

2 Try balancing the clown on your fingertip. Maneuver the clown on your fingertip until you locate its center of gravity. You'll find it's probably near the tip of the clown's chin. Will it balance on the pencil eraser? A pencil tip?

3 Figure out where to tape the pennies so the clown balances with **counterweights**. They should be in the exact same place on opposite sides. Do you think it will be better to tape pennies on the hands or feet? Explain your thinking. Then test it. And be sure to use the same amount of tape with each penny because the tape's weight impacts balance.

4 If you can't get the clown to balance, use trial and error. Adjust the pennies and re-tape them until you find the "sweet spot."

5 Turn the chairs back-to-back. Cut off a length of string and tie it between the chair backs to make a tightrope. Adjust the chairs to keep the string taut. Predict whether the clown will balance on the string and test your prediction.

WORDS to KNOW

counterweights: equal weights that cause an object to be balanced.

Wind Power Windsock

Supplies: *scissors, empty oatmeal container, glue, construction paper, tissue paper, stapler, paper puncher, string*

A windsock is a tube-like device that detects wind direction. Build your own windsock to observe the effects of the wind.

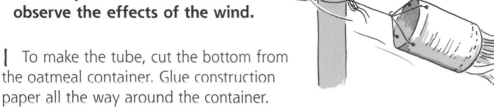

1 To make the tube, cut the bottom from the oatmeal container. Glue construction paper all the way around the container.

2 Cut out long strips of tissue paper for streamers. Glue them to the inside of the container so they dangle out one end. Staple the streamers to the container for extra reinforcement and strength.

3 At the opposite end from the streamers, punch four holes into the container. Cut two lengths of string about 12 inches long (30 centimeters). To make a handle, thread one piece of string through two of the holes and tie it securely. Repeat with the other piece.

4 Cut another length of string about 18 inches (46 centimeters) long. Loop one end through the other two pieces and tie a knot. Go outdoors and tie the other end of the string to a pole, post, or tree limb. Predict how the windsock will respond in the wind. Observe it under a variety of conditions. What happens when wind flows into the tube? How does the windsock respond when wind is calm, moderate, and strong?

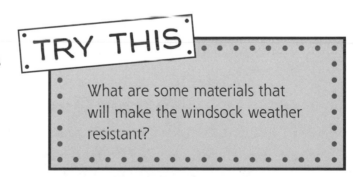

TRY THIS

What are some materials that will make the windsock weather resistant?

Candle Seesaw

Supplies: *knitting needle, cork, 2 candles of equal size, 2 darning needles, 2 glasses of equal size, 2 saucers, matches*

All objects have weight because gravity's force pulls them toward the earth's surface. An object's weight impacts its center of gravity. Work with a **lever** to demonstrate a shifting center of gravity that teeters! **CAUTION:** Have an adult help you to push the knitting needle through the cork. Adult supervision is required when using matches.

WORDS to KNOW

lever: a simple machine made of a rigid bar that pivots on a support, called a fulcrum.

fulcrum: the point on which a lever turns or pivots.

1 Construct the mini seesaw by carefully pushing the knitting needle through the cork's entire width. Then push the knitting needle through the bottom of one candle, opposite the wick end. Press the needle into the candle lengthwise. Push the opposite end of the knitting needle lengthwise into the bottom of the second candle. The cork and candles should be connected in a horizontal beam.

2 Build a **fulcrum** by carefully pushing a darning needle into the middle of each end of the cork. Turn the two glasses upside down. Place them side-by-side to form supports, and place the darning needles across the glasses.

Notable Quotable

"No great discovery was ever made without a bold guess."
—*Isaac Newton (1642–1727), English physicist and mathematician who formulated the three laws of motion*

3 Maneuver the candles into position until the seesaw balances. It will take tweaking to make the seesaw steady. With the candles unlit, you can observe balance.

4 Now position the saucers under the candle wicks to collect wax drippings. Predict what will happen when you light the candles. Light one wick, and when wax begins to drip, light the second wick. Observe the seesaw. Which end dips first? What happens as wax dribbles? How does the center of gravity shift? How does the changing weight of the candles impact center of gravity?

5 Continue your observations until both flames burn out. You probably noticed that as wax drips at one end, center of gravity shifts. It moves to the opposite end. Dripping wax changes the weight of both candles, making the seesaw's center of gravity shift from side to side. The seesaw demonstrates Newton's third law of motion. For every action, there is an equal and opposite reaction. The first dribble of wax is the action. With the seesaw's swinging upward motion, you observe an equal and opposite reaction.

DID YOU KNOW?

The 1989 earthquake rocked San Francisco during the World Series. It occurred shortly before the start of game 3 between the San Francisco Giants and Oakland A's. As tremors jolted Candlestick Park, startled TV viewers across the United States gawked. Network sports coverage broadcast the quake's vibrations live! On ABC news, sportscaster Tim McCarver cried, "I'll tell you what. We're having an earth—." For a confused moment, eerie static seized control of TV screens. Later, the game was nicknamed the Earthquake Series. You can google it! Watch a broadcast of the 1989 World Series as the quake strikes to see an infamous sports moment.

STORY BY STORY: BUILDING UP

STORY BY STORY, PAST CIVILIZATIONS CONSTRUCTED tall structures that reveal a lot about the history of where they are located. Today, many of these amazing structures survive. They are works of art, as well as symbols of the cultural, religious, and political influences that inspired their construction. For example, Horyu-ji is one of Japan's oldest structures. Made of precious wood, its five-story Buddhist temple was first built in the year 607, just after Buddhism was introduced to Japan.

San Gimignano, Italy, is known as "the town of fine towers." Its tower houses became status symbols as local families competed with each other to build taller and taller houses. The town of Shibam, in the country of Yemen, is known for its impressive mud-brick skyscrapers that date back to the sixteenth century, many of which are still inhabited today.

These places are UNESCO World Heritage Sites. UNESCO is the United Nations Educational, Scientific and Cultural Organization. When a structure or place is named a UNESCO World Heritage Site, it brings greater awareness from people inside and outside the country to the importance of preserving the property. There is also money available from the World Heritage Fund to maintain these global treasures. These sites offer insights into past cultures, architecture, and engineering. We learn what people valued, what they honored, and what they feared. We learn how they protected themselves and how they thrived. We discover their feats of engineering.

HORYU-JI TEMPLE COMPLEX: RELIGIOUS ARCHITECTURE

- **Location:** Japan's Nara Prefecture
- **Construction Date:** first temple completed about 607 CE
- **Building Material:** wood

Ancient civilizations expressed spiritual beliefs through religious architecture. These structures provided a community's most sacred, striking buildings. Monuments, temples, and churches were sources of inspiration and respect. The Horyu-ji Temple complex is one of Japan's most cherished monuments. It's also a feat of timber engineering.

The post-and-lintel construction is comprised of two vertical columns, or posts, that support a horizontal beam, or lintel. Intricate bracketing transfers the weight of the heavy tiled roof down to massive supporting columns.

DID YOU KNOW?

Stonehenge still stands tall with post-and-lintel construction. How did ancient laborers hoist these enormous stones? Modern-day experiments revealed that around 2250 BCE, laborers probably used a gigantic wooden lever and timber **scaffolding**.

WORDS to KNOW

scaffolding: a temporary wooden platform used to support construction workers.

entasis: a bulge in a column's shaft, which creates a slight curvature.

optical illusion: a trick of the eyes that makes people see something differently than it really is.

The Horyu-ji Temple complex is known for two distinct architectural traits. First, temple pillars feature **entasis**. By putting a slight bulge in each column, entasis corrects an **optical illusion** that makes a building with perfectly straight sides look like it's caving in. Second, cloud-shaped brackets combine function and beauty, supporting roofs and transferring weight.

Many of the world's oldest surviving wooden structures are here. Among them is the five-story Sai-in pagoda. A pagoda is a slender tiered tower with curving narrow roofs, usually built for religious purposes.

Like a giant puzzle, the magnificent Buddhist pagoda is constructed of interlocking wooden pieces.

There are no nails, and no metal pieces reinforce it. The Sai-in pagoda has proved to be remarkably earthquake proof, remaining undamaged in a seismically active region.

How has a 107-foot (33-meter), 305-ton pagoda survived earthquakes and violent storms? An ancient engineer was a genius of design! The trick is in the pagoda's bendy material and intricate building method.

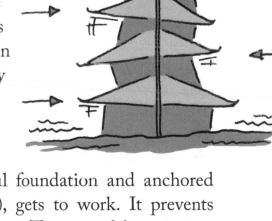

The pagoda's five tiers are structurally independent from one another. A central pillar, called the *shinbashira*, stands on a base stone. It extends up to the spire, but the *shinbashira* doesn't support the structure's roof or framework. It supports no part of the structure! When an earthquake slams the pagoda, a slithery dance starts. The first story, loose on its joints, sways to the right. The second rocks to the left, and so on.

The *shinbashira*, planted in a powerful foundation and anchored almost 10 feet below ground (3 meters), gets to work. It prevents the rocking from toppling the structure. The pagoda's swinging floors counterbalance one another like a huge lever.

DID YOU KNOW?

When scientists studied the tree growth rings of the Sai-in pagoda's timbers, they determined that an ancient lumberjack chopped down the *hinoki*, a Japanese cypress, in 594 CE! The flexibility of timber under tension and compression has kept the pagoda standing. But timber has a fatal flaw. It burns. In 670 CE, a lighting strike triggered a fire that devoured the original buildings of the Horyu-ji Temple complex. Determined ancient engineers began rebuilding almost immediately.

SAN GIMIGNANO'S TOWERS: PROSPERITY, POWER, PROTECTION

- **Location:** Tuscany, Italy
- **Construction Date:** twelfth century CE
- **Building Material:** stone

WORDS to KNOW

medieval: the period of time in European history from about 350 CE to about 1450 CE. Also called the Middle Ages.

The walled town of San Gimignano is nicknamed the **Medieval** Manhattan. Another UNESCO World Heritage Site, it's a stunning example of medieval architecture.

Notable Quotable

"World Heritage sites belong to all the peoples of the world, irrespective of the territory on which they are located."
—*UNESCO World Heritage*

During the Middle Ages, the flourishing town was an important crossroads for **pilgrims** journeying to and from Rome. They rested from their travels in San Gimignano where they also connected with other pilgrims. A center of bustling trade, the town boasted so much wealth and success that thieves attacked it repeatedly. As protection against invaders, the town was fortified with walls, and wealthy families constructed stone tower houses.

WORDS to KNOW

pilgrim: a traveler on a journey to a holy place.

patrician: a member of one of ancient Rome's wealthiest families.

The towers were weighty and sturdy. But the rooms were dark with only a few windows since more would have weakened the strength of the stone walls.

Two rival families, the Ardinghelli and the Salvucci, controlled the town. Over time, clashes between these **patrician** families intensified. To show off their status to the entire town, these competitors built higher and higher tower homes, some soaring to 230 feet tall (70 meters).

DID YOU KNOW?

Locals cherish the distinctive skyline of San Gimignano della Belle Torri, which means "San Gimignano with the beautiful towers." Today, 14 of the original towers survive, including the 177-foot-high Torre Grossa, built in 1311 (54 meters), which visitors can climb for a fantastic view of the town and the countryside.

SHIBAM: CITY PLANNING THROUGH VERTICAL CONSTRUCTION

- **Location:** Shibam, Yemen
- **Construction Date:** sixteenth century CE
- **Building Material:** mud brick

The world's oldest city of skyscrapers is nicknamed Chicago of the Desert or Manhattan of the Desert. Constructed primarily during the sixteenth century, its skyline is modern. Apartment buildings rise from mountain cliffs in the walled city of Shibam. Some stand 100 feet tall (30 meters). Perched on a hilltop, apartments were built of sun-dried mud bricks formed with local clay.

Shibam is a stunning expression of traditional Arab and Muslim culture.

It seems to miraculously rise from a floodplain. Its layout is dense. Streets are narrow. Tightly clustered together, its high rises allowed many people to live in one location. From a distance, its buildings appear to be one behemoth structure.

The ingenious arrangement offered protection. It tricked wandering attackers from descending on the city.

Mud construction is no longer used in the region because it requires constant maintenance and can be wiped out by flooding and **erosion**. In 1532–1533, floodwaters wore away the foundations and some structures collapsed. Flooding in 2008 toppled more buildings. Engineers of the past and present rebuilt the city. Today's residents cover facades with sealants to protect Shibam's buildings from weathering.

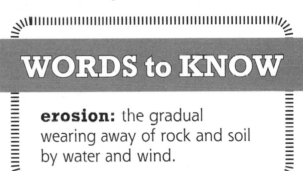

WORDS to KNOW

erosion: the gradual wearing away of rock and soil by water and wind.

IMPERFECT PYRAMID

What do you see when you visualize an Egyptian pyramid? You probably picture the "classic" shape—smooth, sloped sides with a pointed top. The first attempt to construct a pyramid didn't go exactly as planned. Around 2600 BCE, the Egyptian king, Pharaoh Snefru, ordered construction of a smooth pyramid with very steep sides.

Structural problems plagued construction from the beginning. Built on weak, sandy soil, the pyramid tilted and leaned into itself at an unsafe angle. Builders feared the pyramid would collapse under its own weight so they abandoned the project.

EL CASTILLO

Surviving step pyramids, like the massive Ziggurat of Ur, can be found around the world. Among these is the 79-foot El Castillo (24 meters), a spectacular stone Maya temple that was built around 1000 CE in Chichen Itza. This incredible archaeological site lies in the Yucatán peninsula of present-day Mexico. It's a gigantic Maya calendar! Each of El Castillo's four faces contains extremely steep stairways of 91 steps. All four faces share one step at the top of the pyramid. That's a total of 365 steps, to match the number of days in a year.

El Castillo is famous for its serpents. Carved diamond-back snakes with gaping mouths flank its stone stairways. Every year at the equinoxes, crowds gather and cheer at nature's breathtaking special effects. As the sun falls, the pyramid's steps cast triangular shadows. Serpents seem to spring to life in the stone. Rippling snakes appear to slither down the pyramid's stairway!

Notable Quotable

"Imagination is more important than knowledge."
—*Albert Einstein*

After erecting other structures and learning valuable lessons through trial and error, Egyptian engineers resumed construction on what is known today as the Bent Pyramid. They made it less steep, reducing its angle from 60 to 55 degrees, and enlarged the base to make the structure more stable. It didn't work. They changed the angle again, this time to 43 degrees. But soon they abandoned the crooked pyramid—for the second time. Why? British Egyptologist John Romer theorizes that builders heard horrible groans. The creaking pyramid cried out like a living thing. Terrified of collapse, laborers fled.

WORDS to KNOW

buttress: a support that adds stability to a wall or building.

After successfully building the Red Pyramid, Egyptian builders tried for a third time to save the Bent Pyramid. They set huge stone blocks that added stability and built **buttresses** to support the structure. They sank giant foundation stones into gravelly soil to combat the weak foundation. The Bent Pyramid was still crooked, but it stood high and stable. These determined engineers paved the way for the truly classic pyramids that followed.

DID YOU KNOW?

Due to the rebuilding efforts, the Bent Pyramid is one of Egypt's best-preserved pyramids.

Build a Sand Tower

Supplies: *large plastic tub, sand, water, large bucket with the bottom cut out, spade, measuring spoons, spatula*

Design and construct a tapered sand tower with a sturdy foundation. Can you keep it from toppling? If you try this at the beach, you can dig the tower's foundation right into the sand.

1 Fill the tub with sand. In the middle, press the sand with your hands to construct a sturdy foundation for the tower.

COMPACTED SAND FOUNDATION

2 Build a tower on top of the foundation. Place the bucket on the foundation, with the open end up. Gradually fill the bucket with sand and water to form a tower. What is the most effective sand-to-water ratio? How much sand and water will be required to keep the base from crumbling? From leaking? To keep the tower vertical? Too much water will weaken the foundation. Too little will make the sand hard to compact. Continue to add sand and water as you build up. Mix and press the sand with your hands. Construct a solid tower all the way to the open end of the bucket.

3 Quickly flip the bucket over onto the foundation. Gently remove the bucket. Be careful not to knock over your tower.

DID YOU KNOW?

Ed Jarrett holds a Guinness World's Record for the tallest sandcastle. Jarrett used 1.6 million pounds of sand to build a sandcastle 37 feet, 10 inches high (11½ meters)! Like all big structures, construction required cooperation. He had 1,500 volunteers pitch in to help.

4 With your hands, build a sand base on top of the tower. From the base, construct a tapered section.

5 With the spoons, scoop sand away from the tower, creating windows of different sizes. Use the spatula to etch designs into the tower.

6 Assess your structure. Does your tower stand straight and tall? Does it lean? What sand-to-water ratio worked best?

TRY THIS

How can you build a sand castle that is more stable? What did you try? Did it work? Why or why not?

SANDCASTLE SCIENCE

What's the trick to building the perfect sandcastle? The sand-to-water ratio! A sandcastle's strength depends on how sand grains interact.

When a group of physicists studied the science of sandcastles, they conducted experiments to explore ideal building techniques. How could sand and water combine to build steep angles? They found that one part water to 50 parts sand gave the highest strength, and that densely compacted sand creates stronger castles. And the best technique for compressing sand? Your hands!

The Right Footing

Supplies: *marker, 4 paper cups, dirt, gravel, mud, sand, 4 craft sticks, blow dryer with multiple settings, science journal and pencil, water*

A pagoda's tiers hold up to the force of powerful winds by moving independently. Shibam's mud skyrises also stand up to the force of wind. But Shibam is vulnerable to floods. Experiment with natural materials to build foundations, determining which best stand up to the forces of wind and water.

1 Label each of the paper cups: Dirt, Gravel, Mud, Sand. Fill the cups halfway with the materials indicated. Each represents a different ground condition on which a tower will be built. Tamp down each material with your fingertips to compact it.

2 Firmly plant a craft stick in each cup. Allow each tower to stand for a few minutes. What do you observe? Has there been any movement or leaning? Which tower appears most solidly planted?

DIRT   GRAVEL   MUD   SAND

3 Predict what will happen when you simulate wind's force. At its lowest setting, aim the blow dryer at the flat side of each tower in turn. How does each respond? What happens when you switch to higher settings? Record your observations on the data chart.

Dirt	Gravel	Mud	Sand
Low Wind Trial:	Low Wind Trial:	Low Wind Trial:	Low Wind Trial:
High Wind Trial:	High Wind Trial:	High Wind Trial:	High Wind Trial:
Flood Trial:	Flood Trial:	Flood Trial:	Flood Trial:

4 Predict what will happen when you simulate flooding. How will each foundation hold up? How will each tower respond? Pour water into each cup until it reaches the top of the foundation. Record your observations on the data chart.

5 Assess your findings. What conclusions can you draw about foundations and forces?

DID YOU KNOW?

The Tiger Hill Pagoda tilts! Officially known as the Huqui Tower of Suzhou, China, the elegant pagoda stands 154 feet tall (47 meters). In about 960 BCE, ancient engineers constructed it with brick and mud. But they erected it on an unstable foundation that is part rock and part soil. The Huqui Tower's top tilts by about 7.6 feet (2.32 meters).

Shaped Strong

Supplies: *scissors, file folders, paper punch, brass fasteners, plastic straws, craft sticks, pipe cleaners, rubber bands*

Skyscrapers evolved from towers. Today, New York's Flatiron Building is an iconic landmark known for its unusual triangular shape. Construct a rectangle and a triangle with strips cut from file folders and brass fasteners. Which shape best resists forces?

1 Cut the folders into eight strips of equal size. Punch holes into the ends of each strip.

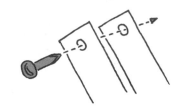

2 Set one strip aside for now. With the other seven strips, construct a rectangle and a triangle. Secure their corners with the fasteners.

3 Test the rectangle's side. Make a prediction. How will the rectangle hold up to pushes? Test your prediction. Push one side with your finger. Is the rectangle stable? Does it hold its shape or slant in the direction you pushed it?

DID YOU KNOW?

The Flatiron Building was completed in 1902. Its name comes from its shape, like an iron you use to press your clothes. Today, the Flatiron Building is beloved for its unique look. But one early detractor snarked that it resembled a "stingy piece of pie." Its famous shape produces wild gusts of wind at street level. This gives the Flatiron Building its own microclimate!

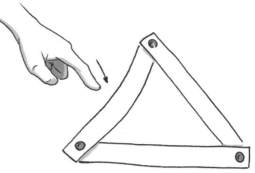

4 Test the triangle. Predict how it will hold up when you push one side. Test your predictions. Press one side with your finger. What happens? The side you pushed compresses, or squishes together. At the same time, the inside edge pulls apart. It's experiencing tension. So the triangle experiences compression and tension simultaneously. These forces cause the side to bend. Why? A triangle is weakest at its sides.

5 Predict what will happen when you press the triangle's top. Push your finger down. How does the triangle hold up? You probably find it remains stable. It stays rigid. Why? As you push, the two sides squeeze together under compression and the bottom side pulls apart under tension. Each side experiences only one force at a time. Triangles are the strongest geometric shapes. They stay stable because they can't be distorted. What happens when you press down on the rectangle?

TRY THIS

You've tested shapes and explored their strengths and weaknesses. Now, head back to the drawing board. Use the remaining materials and trial and error to figure out how to reinforce your shapes for extra strength and stability. Where are the weak areas? Can you strengthen those areas by adding more material? How can you position more pieces of file folder for added strength?

Test your redesigned shapes for strengths and weaknesses. Do they hold up to more force than before?

Sugar Cube Step Pyramid

Supplies: *sturdy sheet of cardboard, sugar cubes, glue, ruler*

The ancient Egyptians learned from their building mistakes to successfully construct the pyramids. Step pyramids were temple towers built of stone platforms gradually decreasing in size. Steps rose from the ground up to the apex, at the very top. Construct a step pyramid on a cardboard base.

1 Construct a square base on the cardboard, arranging rows of 10 sugar cubes across and 10 down. Attach the cubes to the cardboard using glue. Use the ruler as a guide to build straight lines.

2 Build the second level, arranging 9 cubes across and 9 down.

3 Continue building each level smaller than the level beneath it by decreasing the number of cubes in the rows by one. A single cube forms the apex. Use trial and error to determine how far in to position the rising levels to maintain the pyramid's shape.

4 Assess your construction. How many cubes did you use in total? How effectively does the structure resemble a geometric pyramid?

TRY THIS

Ancient ziggurat builders relied on sun-baked mud. How can you modify your building materials to construct a stronger structure? What was the most difficult part of construction? The easiest?

CHICAGO: SKY HIGH IN THE WINDY CITY

FROM THE 1850s UNTIL 1910, THERE WAS A FLURRY of invention and innovation. New technologies brought incredible changes to the construction of tall structures. Steel-frame construction, electricity, and braking elevators all made modern skyscrapers possible.

Chicago is known as the birthplace of skyscrapers. It's hard to imagine that a city with so many impressive vertical structures marking its skyline once saw most of its buildings burn to the ground. Chicago's neck-craning wonders of today dwarf the early buildings that were lost in the Great Chicago Fire. But those first structures towered in importance.

FIRE DEVILS LEAVE A CITY IN RUINS

The fall of 1871 was unusually hot and dry in Chicago. At about 9 pm on October 8, a fire ignited in Patrick and Catherine O'Leary's barn. Winds from the bordering prairies fanned the fire. Gusts triggered **convection** spirals known as fire devils, which look like spinning tornados of fire.

The giant mass of fire produced its own forward motion and circular blazes quickly swirled through Chicago's business district and beyond. Along the way, they threw off sizzling debris, which ignited new flames. Overnight, the inferno devoured most of the prosperous, populous city.

Rainstorms on October 10 finally doused the flames, but Chicago lay in ruins. The fire **ravaged** the city's wooden office buildings, banks, and theaters. It destroyed an astonishing 18,000 structures. Strangely, while the disaster killed at least 300 people and left 100,000 homeless, the O'Leary's barn was not damaged.

WORDS to KNOW

convection: the massive vertical movement of heat or fire.

ravage: to cause severe damage to something.

WOOD BURNS!

According to Chicago legend, the O'Leary's cow kicked over a kerosene lamp and set off the fire. The cow tale is still shared today but don't believe it! It's been confirmed that the fire began in the O'Leary's barn, though the cause of the blaze remains an unsolved mystery of history.

Was this a disaster waiting to happen? At the time, Chicago was the fastest-growing city in America. In just 40 years after its founding in 1837, the population exploded from a town of 150 people to a bustling city of 340,000. Buildings went up fast. The cheapest, quickest building material was timber, so most of the city's factories, shops, houses, and schools were built of wood. Even its sidewalks were made with wooden planks. The few structures made of brick and stone were trimmed with wood. What's wood's fatal flaw? It burns! So when the Great Chicago Fire started it found a city made to quickly burn to the ground.

Notable Quotable

"Late one night, when we were all in bed,
Old Mother Leary left a lantern in the shed;
When the cow kicked it over, she winked her eye and said,
'There'll be a hot time in the old town, tonight.'"
—*Children's song "Mrs. O'Leary's Cow"*

The people of Chicago immediately united to start the "Great Rebuilding" of their city. After being slowed by a financial crisis and another fire that destroyed more than 800 buildings, eventually, Chicago gave birth to the world's first true skyscraper and changed the future of urban landscapes forever.

DID YOU KNOW?

As people teamed up to rebuild the city, Chicago's real estate market flourished. People snagged property in the heart of the city at a frenzied pace. With Lake Michigan on its east border and the Chicago River on its west, this valuable property was limited. Building out wasn't an option. The only way to go was up!

FIRST MODERN SKYSCRAPER: HOME INSURANCE BUILDING

- **Height:** 138 feet (42 meters)
- **Designed by:** architect and engineer William Le Baron Jenney
- **Completed:** 1885

Architect and engineer William Le Baron Jenney (1832–1907) is called the Father of the American Skyscraper. He designed the Home Insurance Building, which, when completed in 1885, launched a whole new architectural style known as the Chicago School.

The 10-story building was the first modern skyscraper with an all-metal skeleton. Most of the skeleton was made of iron, but Jenney used stronger, lighter steel on the top floors. With steel, the building could be built higher without crumbling under its own weight. The frame was so rigid and stable that walls didn't need to be made of bulky brick and stone. And thinner walls left plenty of room for windows all around to let in natural light. No more dark, gloomy buildings for Chicago!

DID YOU KNOW?

Chicago city officials weren't convinced the Home Insurance Building, with its steel frame and brick facing, would stay standing. They feared it would topple under its own weight. But in 1890, five years after it opened, officials agreed that two more stories could be added, raising the building's height to 180 feet (55 meters).

GLAZED TERRA COTTA SKIN: RELIANCE BUILDING

- **Height:** 201.66 feet (61.46 meters)
- **Designed by:** architects John Root and Charles Atwood
- **Completed:** 1895

On the heels of Jenney's success, the Reliance Building was built in 1895. It shone in Chicago's new skyline as one of the first buildings with electricity. Architects John Root and Charles Atwood designed the 15-story building on a foundation of clay.

The building's sturdy steel skeleton, constructed with a grid of beams and columns, supported forces and loads and allowed plenty of exterior space for windows. Dressed in a facade of glazed terra cotta clay, the building inspired today's glass-and-steel skyscrapers. Although the Home Insurance Building was demolished in 1931, the Reliance Building stands today. Taller structures now dwarf the historical building, yet it remains a giant of achievement.

Chicago's rebirth was so complete that the city hosted the World's Fair in 1893 just 22 years after fire gutted the metropolis!

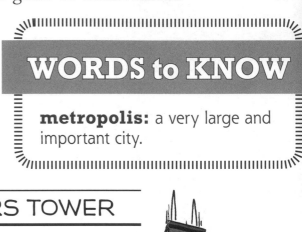

WORDS to KNOW

metropolis: a very large and important city.

BUNDLED TUBES: SEARS TOWER

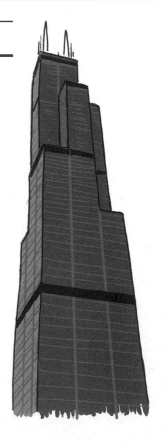

- **Height:** 1,454 feet (442.87 meters)
- **Designed by:** architect and engineer Fazlur Khan of Skidmore, Owings & Merrill
- **Completed:** 1973
- **Building cost:** $150 million (over $785 million in 2013)

Completed in 1973, the Sears Tower was the corporate headquarters of Sears Roebuck & Co., then the world's largest retailer. It briefly reigned as the world's tallest building, until the Petronas Towers dethroned it in 1997. Today, the Sears Tower has been renamed Willis Tower. But you won't find many Chicagoans who call it by that name!

Though Sears Tower long ago lost its title as the world's tallest skyscraper, it still remains North America's tallest building.

Architect and engineer Fazlur Khan designed Sears Tower as a bundle of nine square towers, or "tubes," all soaring at different heights. Instead of clustering the beams and columns that support each tower in the center, Khan placed them along the outer walls. This turned each tower into a highly wind-resistant hollow tube. By grouping the tubes together, he gave the skyscraper its unique, multi-level appearance in Chicago's skyline.

CHICAGO'S AQUA

Chicago's skyline continues to evolve. In 2010, architect Jeanne Gang unveiled the dazzling 82-story Aqua. Aqua is the tallest building in the world to be designed with a woman as the lead architect. With curvy concrete balconies that seem to ripple like the waves of Lake Michigan that inspired it, Aqua appears more like a sculpture than a building.

As *The New York Times* described it, "the building seems to flutter with the winds that gust off nearby Lake Michigan. Yet Aqua's beautiful skin is not just for show. The balconies block the sun's rays and slice through breezes, allowing residents to venture outdoors at heights unprecedented in Chicago."

On the day the Sears Tower was scheduled for completion, the Windy City lived up to its nickname. The *Chicago Tribune* described how powerful gusts nearly derailed the event.

"A final 2,500-pound girder was lifted a quarter mile into the sky yesterday to make the Sears Tower the world's tallest building. It almost didn't come about. Strong winds threatened to delay the topping off of the building. It was feared the heavy beam would break some windows on its way to the top. But the strong, cold winds seemed to die down just long enough for the lifting as dignitaries below stretched their necks upward and a chorus of hardhat electrical workers sang these lyrics: *She towers so high – Just scraping the sky – She's the tallest rock*."

DID YOU KNOW?

On a clear day, you can see four midwestern states from Willis Tower's Skydeck—Illinois, Indiana, Michigan, and Wisconsin!

Willis Tower is a city in the sky. It even has its own zip code!

CITY MOUNTAIN CLIMBER

Stuntman Alain Robert, known as the French Spiderman, has scaled most of the world's tallest skyscrapers and monuments without ropes or climbing gear! Wearing climbing shoes and using only his hands, Robert ascended the Willis, Petronas, and Eiffel Towers, as well as the Sydney Opera House. As a rock climber, Robert was inspired by the sheer height of Chicago's structures. He wrote in his autobiography, *With Bare Hands*, "The city of Chicago had just opened a door to a whole new universe, a range of mountains of steel and glass."

GOING UP!

Vertical structures need vertical transportation. Trudging up flights and flights of stairs isn't practical, especially in buildings bursting with thousands of occupants. Do you think skyscrapers would be possible without elevators?

In 1852, inventor Elisha Graves Otis **patented** elevator safety brakes. Elevators were already used to hoist **cargo**, but the safety brake allowed elevators to move people. The safety mechanism inspired engineers and architects to aim high, building bigger and taller. In 1880, German inventor Werner Von Siemens constructed the first electric elevator.

WORDS to KNOW

patent: having the exclusive right to make, use, or sell something.

cargo: a load of something.

incandescent: containing a wire that glows when heated by an electric current.

filament: the wire thread in an electric bulb that glows when heated by a current.

DID YOU KNOW?

What's the greatest invention of all? Many believe it's electricity. This vital part of our world powers computers, lights homes, and runs appliances. It's hard to imagine life without it. In 1879, Thomas Edison invented the **incandescent** light bulb, which hasn't changed much since. Edison's bulb contained a **filament** that glowed when electricity passed through it. By 1881, he devised and built New York City's first electrical power and distribution center. Today's skyscrapers rely on electrical systems for power and communication.

For thousands of years, people have devised clever ways to move things from one level to another. Ancient Greeks lifted objects using a rotating drum with ropes coiled around it. With weights and pulleys, people hoisted baskets and nets loaded with goods. Farmers used donkeys and waterwheels to raise and lower bulky loads. During the Industrial Revolution, steam powered platform elevators in factories and mines. But these elevators were dangerous and hoisting goods on them was risky. A snapped cable brought disaster.

Otis devised a brake that worked automatically if a cable snapped. In 1854, he used high drama to introduce his spectacular new creation at New York's Crystal Palace Exposition. His curious audience jammed the main exhibition hall. Today's Otis Elevator Company recalls the historic event. "In the main exhibition hall, Otis constructed a complete safety elevator equipped with guiderails, ratchets, a spring, a platform, and hoisting machinery. Otis had the hoist fully loaded with freight . . . He climbed on the platform and ordered it raised to full height. The hoisting rope was cut with an axe. The crowd gasped. But before the platform could fall, the safety spring locked the lift in place as Otis reassured the crowd with the cry, 'All safe, gentlemen. All safe.'"

DID YOU KNOW?

When New York's One World Trade Center opens in 2013, it will boast the Western Hemisphere's five speediest elevators. They'll soar to the top of the skyscraper at 2,000 feet in one minute (609 meters)!

WILLIS TOWER'S SKYDECK

Scramble onto the Ledge, if you dare! You're sky high, perched on a glass floor 103 stories above downtown Chicago. Your fingertips press a clear wall. Your forehead smudges cool glass. You peer down at a **panoramic** view from a **cantilevered** glass balcony 1,353 feet above the ground (412 meters). Beneath a glass walkway, the city sprawls at your feet. Chicago looks like a map brought to life. People swarm like ants at a picnic along the busy sidewalks below. Your heart pounds. Welcome to the enormously popular Willis Tower Skydeck Ledge. It's a must-do for locals and tourists alike!

When the new owners of the Sears Tower changed its name to Willis Tower in 2009, they were eager to tweak the skyscraper's image. What would make the Skydeck even more thrilling for visitors? The architects turned to experts in structural glass design who came up with an almost-invisible support system for four glass observation boxes that extend over four feet out from the side of the building. These glass balconies provide the skyscraper's 1.3 million yearly visitors an exhilarating, heart-stopping experience.

WORDS to KNOW

panoramic: a wide, unobstructed view in all directions.

cantilevered: a projected structure attached or supported only on one end.

DID YOU KNOW?

The popular 1986 movie *Ferris Bueller's Day Off* was filmed in Chicago. When high school student Ferris ditches class to hang out downtown with his friends, their first stop is the Skydeck!

Notable Quotable

Sloane: "The city looks so peaceful from up here."
Ferris: "Anything is peaceful from one thousand, three hundred, and fifty-four feet."
—*Ferris Bueller's Day Off*

Triangular Bracing

Supplies: *pipe cleaners, plastic coffee stirrers—5-inch and 7-inch sizes (12.7 and 17.5 centimeters), scissors, file folder, magazine, slim paperback book*

Chicago's 1,000-foot-tall John Hancock Center (305 meters) features huge diagonal X-braces on its exterior. They provide stability and wind resistance in the Windy City, where the average wind speed is 16 miles per hour (almost 26 kilometers per hour). You can see how the triangles made by X-bracing help stabilize the structure. Build a tower with coffee stirrers and pipe cleaners and reinforce it with triangular bracing.

1 Assess your building materials. When you push, pull, and twist the pipe cleaners and coffee stirrers, how do they respond to compression, tension, and torsion? Are they strong enough for construction? Make predictions about the materials.

2 You'll use the pipe cleaners as connectors between the stirrers at the corners, so cut them into smaller sections.

3 Construct the building's base with four short stirrers and four pieces of pipe cleaner. Test the base by pushing and pulling it. What happens? You probably notice you can distort it easily and shape-shift it into a slanted square.

Notable Quotable
"By day the skyscraper looms in the smoke and sun and has a soul."
—*Carl Sandburg (1878–1967)*
Pulitzer Prize–winning American poet and author

4 Now divide the square base into two triangles to make a trussed frame. Use two connectors and one longer, 7-inch stirrer. How can you make this work? Use trial and error to find the length you need to trim the stirrer to make a supportive brace. How can you best position the brace for added strength?

5 Test the trussed frame. What happens when you push and pull it? How does it differ from the untrussed base you made earlier?

6 Using only trussed frames, construct a vertical, freestanding structure at least three levels high.

7 Stand your structure on a sturdy surface. Predict how much weight it will support until it collapses. Test the folder, magazine, and paperback in turn. What happens?

DID YOU KNOW?

A skyscraper's lights can form a part of its architecture. Lighting makes skyscrapers pop against a night sky. But illuminated buildings are hazardous for migratory birds that travel at night. Lights confuse birds and they can crash into the building's glass. Twice a year, Chicago's skyscrapers turn off their lights at night, providing safe passage for 5 million migratory birds flying through the city.

Experiment with Electricity

Supplies: *utility knife, #2 pencils, pencil sharpener, scissors, thin cardboard, 1 teaspoon salt, small glass of warm water, spoon, 9-volt battery, electrical wire*

An electrical system is one of the most important inner elements of a skyscraper. Willis Tower has 2,000 miles of electrical wire (3,200 kilometers). Electricity is produced when chemicals react with each other. Create your own chemical reaction! Use a 9-volt battery and wiring to pass an electrical current through a glass of water. CAUTION: This experiment uses a utility knife so ask an adult to help.

1 Ask an adult to use the utility knife to remove the erasers and metal sections from two pencils. Sharpen each pencil at both ends.

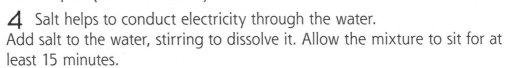

ELECTRICAL WIRES TOUCHING LEAD

2 Cut the cardboard into a rectangular piece that will fit across the opening of the glass.

3 Carefully press the pencils through the cardboard. Position them about 1 inch apart (2½ centimeters).

4 Salt helps to conduct electricity through the water. Add salt to the water, stirring to dissolve it. Allow the mixture to sit for at least 15 minutes.

5 What will happen when you wire the pencils to the battery and place them in water? Make your predictions.

Notable Quotable

"Life is trying things to see if they work."
—*Ray Bradbury, legendary sci-fi author, poet, and playwright*

6   On the battery, locate the positive and negative symbols. Cut two pieces of electrical wire, each a few inches long. Connect one end of one of the wires to the battery's positive side. Connect the other end to one pencil tip.

7   Connect one end of the second piece of wire to the negative side. Connect the other end to the second pencil tip.

8   Both pencils should now be wired to the battery. Test your predictions by placing the unwired pencil ends into the water. Carefully observe what happens. You should see mini bubbles collecting around the submerged pencil tips. Why? An electrical current from the battery passes through and between the tips connected to the battery and the tips submerged in water. The tips are electrodes, which are conductors of electricity. Water splits into hydrogen and chlorine gas. You split water by running electricity through it!

DID YOU KNOW?

Lightning is an electric current. On June 23, 2010, lightning storms rocked downtown Chicago. In the early evening hours, an ominous gray sky hung over the city. Winds gusted to 80 miles per hour (129 kilometers per hour). Thunder rumbled and lightning split the sky. In one incredible instant, jagged bolts struck three of Chicago's tallest skyscrapers—the Willis Tower, John Hancock Center, and Trump International Hotel and Tower. A triple hit!

Spiraling Flame

Supplies: *pencil, 4-by-4-inch piece of paper (10 by 10 centimeters), markers (red, orange, and yellow), scissors, 20 inches of yarn (51 centimeters), safety goggles, desk lamp or small table lamp*

During the Great Chicago Fire, convection spirals swirled over Chicago like blazing tornadoes. Explore the way air molecules move by creating your own convection current that causes a paper coil to swirl. CAUTION: The light bulb can get hot.

1 Draw a spiral pattern on the paper square, and add a dot to the center. Color the paper spiral like a blazing flame, and cut it out along the spiral line.

2 Use the scissors to poke a starter hole through the dot on the flame. Thread the yarn through the underside of the hole. Pull the yarn all the way through the coiled flame. Knot it tightly beneath the flame. Your coiled flame should dangle from the yarn.

3 What will happen when you hold the coiled flame above the light bulb, which is a heat source? Wear the goggles to protect your eyes. Turn on the light. Hold the end of the yarn and dangle the paper flame about 5 inches above the bulb (13 centimeters). Make sure you don't touch the bulb with your fingers or allow the paper flame to touch the bulb.

4 What happens? Energy from the light will cause air molecules to move. The air will become warmer and lighter and move up. Cooler air will move in to replace the rising warmer air. Moving air creates convection currents like the fire devils that swirled over Chicago. Your flame should swirl and spiral like a fire devil.

NEW YORK CITY: VERTICAL METROPOLIS

DURING THE ROARING TWENTIES, AMERICA'S WEALTH DOUBLED.
Cities expanded as new highways, electricity, indoor
plumbing, sewer systems, telephone lines, and automobiles
all contributed to a construction boom. New York grew
to become the world's most populated city. But could the
"Big Apple" outdo Chicago's impressive skyscrapers?

Because New York City is surrounded by water, engineers had
to maximize space. So they built up and up and up, launching
a fierce height competition. The flurry of one-upping resulted in
Manhattan's famous skyline.

SNEAKY SPIRE: CHRYSLER BUILDING

- **Height:** 1,046 feet (319 meters)
- **Designed by:** architect William Van Alen
- **Completed:** 1930
- **Building cost:** $20 million (equal to over $278 million in 2013)

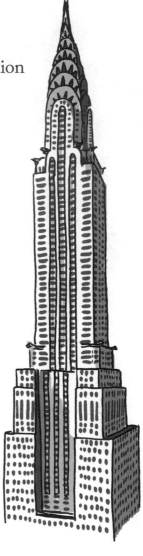

The mad scramble to reach for the skies triggered a dramatic engineering stunt. In the summer of 1929, a race was on in New York's financial district to construct the world's tallest building. At the time, the Eiffel Tower in Paris held the title, standing 986 feet tall (300 meters).

Two contenders competed head-to-head. Would the Chrysler Building or the Bank of Manhattan come out on top? To curious outside eyes, it looked like the Bank of Manhattan would win the race. But auto **tycoon** Walter Chrysler had other plans. He had hired architect William Van Alen to design his dream building, a structure that would be an eye-opening contribution to the modern age. Chrysler wanted the building to command attention and make his cars famous.

WORDS to KNOW

tycoon: a wealthy, powerful person in business or industry.

When Chrysler feared that his building might not be the tallest, he told his architect, "Van, you've just got to get up and do something . . . It looks as if we're not going to be the highest."

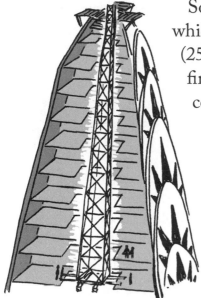

So Van Alen added a steel arch to the structure, which raised the skyscraper from 840 to 860 feet (256 to 262 meters). And inside the building's lofty fire shaft, the ingenious architect's workers began constructing a steel spire in secret.

They waited until the Bank of Manhattan topped out at 927 feet (282 meters). A week later, Van Alen revealed his hidden tip as workers hoisted the shiny spire into position. In 90 minutes the building gained 186 feet (57 meters) to reach 1,046 feet (319 meters), surpassing the Eiffel Tower, the Bank of Manhattan, and all of Chicago's tallest buildings.

The Chrysler Building victory didn't last long. Just 11 months later the Empire State Building was completed and seized the crown.

WORDS to KNOW

ornate: elaborately decorated.

replica: an exact copy of something.

DID YOU KNOW?

The Chrysler Building is a masterpiece of the Art Deco style of architecture. The steel skyscraper features **ornate**, zigzag geometric shapes, and its glitzy structure even includes **replicas** of the hood ornaments that were being used on Chrysler cars in 1929! The building is clad in dark gray and white brick. Its sneaky spire is decked out with an elaborate sunburst pattern.

GAPING GARGOYLES

Gargoyles are fascinating architectural elements that have been used since ancient times. In ancient Egyptian architecture, they usually looked like a long lion's head jutting out from a building. But later, they took on all sorts of strange combinations of humans and animals, and were often meant to be funny. With channels carved along their backs and gaping or roaring mouths, gargoyles are more than just decorative and fun to observe. They're an artistic solution to a problem. Rainwater collects in these channels and gushes from their mouths, away from the structure. Gargoyles prevent water from running down the structure's face and eroding its terra cotta or stone surface. If you ever visit the Notre Dame cathedral in Paris, you'll see some great gargoyles!

WORDS to KNOW

gargoyle: an architectural element that serves as a rainspout, often in the form of distorted humans and animals.

Gargoyle **comes from the French word** *gargouille*, **or "throat." It probably originated from the rainspouts' gargling sounds!**

The glamorous Chrysler Building pulled out all the stops in its design. The skyscraper's exterior decorations are dazzling, with amazing steel gargoyles that are different from traditional stone carvings. On some corners of the building, magnificent eagles jut out and peer over the city. Other corners feature winged radiator caps and flying hubcaps!

RECORD TIME AND LIFTED SPIRITS: EMPIRE STATE BUILDING

- **Height:** 1,250 feet (381 meters)
- **Designed by:** architect William F. Lamb
- **Completed:** 1931
- **Building cost:** $41 million (equal to over $627 million in 2013)

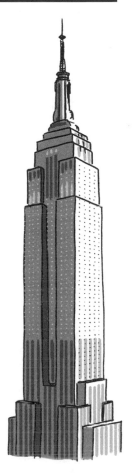

What's the most famous building in the world? Many believe it's the Empire State Building, symbol of both New York City and the United States.

During the Great Depression of the 1930s, construction offered great opportunities for employment. Over 3,000 workers toiled every day, including weekends and holidays. This speedy race for the sky racked up 7 million hours of labor! After erecting the frame, laborers built one floor each day, completing construction on the 365,000-ton skyscraper in just one year and 45 days.

DID YOU KNOW?

The American Society of Civil Engineers (ASCE) named the Empire State Building one of the Seven Wonders of the Modern World. The ASCE created the list as "a tribute to modern society's ability to achieve the unachievable, reach unreachable heights, and scorn the notion of 'it can't be done.'" More than 90 movies feature the Empire State Building! The 1933 film King Kong and its 2005 remake are among the most famous.

This steel skyscraper with clean, vertical lines and a granite face opened during a time when many Americans were out of work. They struggled to make ends meet. The Empire State Building was a symbol of the hopes and dreams that boosted the nation's spirits. The skyscraper reigned as tallest of the tall for 41 years until the World Trade Center Twin Towers took the title in 1972.

DID YOU KNOW?

At the top of the Empire State Building, snow doesn't always fall down. It falls up! The skyscraper creates its own microclimate. Wind currents around it alter snow's direction. An updraft blasts snow upward.

FALLEN GIANTS: WORLD TRADE CENTER TWIN TOWERS

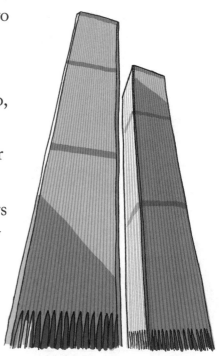

- **Height:** Tower One 1,368 feet; Tower Two 1,362 feet

- **Designed by:** architect Minoru Yamasaki

- **Completed:** Tower One, 1972; Tower Two, 1973

- **Building cost:** $400 million (equal to over $2 billion in 2013)

At completion, the steel-and-glass Twin Towers became the world's tallest buildings. They reigned only briefly until Chicago's Sears Tower became champ in 1974. Soaring over the heart of New York's bustling financial district, the Twin Towers symbolized power and wealth. Over 50,000 people worked inside them.

SUSTAINABLE HEARST TOWER

New York's 46-story, steel-and-glass Hearst Tower is the city's first "green" building. *Travel and Leisure* magazine named the **sustainable** structure one of the World's Most Beautiful Buildings. Its interior is drenched with light from windows with spectacular views of Central Park. With a honeycombed facade of slanted glass, Hearst Tower resembles a gargantuan faceted gem!

WORDS to KNOW

sustainable: able to continue with little effect on the environment.

settlement load: a change in soil as a mammoth structure settles into the ground.

Engineers designed the World Trade Center towers to withstand mammoth loads. In the land-strapped metropolis, the buildings sat atop an old landfill. Engineers anchored the huge skyscrapers in bedrock 70 feet underground (21 meters). The deep foundation allowed the buildings to withstand **settlement loads** as the skyscrapers' enormous weight pressed into the ground. Built of tubes strengthened with columns and beams, the skyscrapers were able to resist the load of hurricane-force winds.

70 FEET

Minoru Yamasaki, architect of the World Trade Center Twin Towers, had a fear of heights! He designed the structures with small windows. He believed small windows offered occupants a sense of security.

Though the mighty structures stood up to a terrorist truck bomb in 1993, they completely collapsed during the September 11 attacks

DID YOU KNOW?

In 1974, it took French aerialist Philippe Petit 45 minutes to walk 250 feet (76 meters) across a tightrope strung between New York's Twin Towers 1,300 feet above ground (396 meters).

in 2001. Why? When the hijacked planes slammed into the twin structures, each building caught on fire. Extreme heat from the fires weakened the skyscrapers' support structures. In a domino effect, the upper floors collapsed. Then floor upon floor plunged onto lower levels. Crushing loads overwhelmed each lower floor.

With the nation glued to its television sets, the Twin Towers tumbled before our eyes. Residents of New York City, together with people all around the world, were in a state of shock.

FREEDOM TOWER

Today, 12 years after the world watched the World Trade Center Twin Towers crumble, One World Trade Center is one of the structures being erected on its site. Also known as the Freedom Tower, the completed building will be 1,776 feet tall (541 meters). The height is a symbolic reference to America's year of independence, 1776. This makes it the tallest building in the Western Hemisphere and the third-highest building in the world, behind Dubai's Burj Khalifa (2,717 feet or 828 meters) and Mecca's Makkah Royal Clock Tower Hotel (1,972 feet or 601 meters).

Eggstraordinary Pressure

Supplies: *hard-boiled egg (peeled), glass bottle, newspaper, matches*

In 1888, Theophilus Van Kannel patented the revolving door in the United States. This now-familiar entrance to modern skyscrapers prevents drafts and collisions. Otherwise cold air would be sucked into a building's lobby and blow everything around! Experiment using air pressure to suck an egg into a bottle and you'll see how strong it can be. CAUTION: This project uses matches, so ask an adult to help.

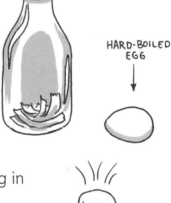

1 Carefully choose an egg-and-bottle combination. You'll have the most success with an egg that is close in size to the bottle's mouth or a little larger. A small milk jug works well.

NEWSPAPER STRIPS

HARD-BOILED EGG

2 Place the bottle on a steady surface. Insert strips of newspaper into it. Ask an adult to help you light the paper with a match. You may need several matches to get the paper to ignite.

3 When the paper starts to burn, quickly place the egg in the bottle's neck.

4 Observe the egg. Predict what will happen as you wait. How long do you think it will take to observe a change? What happens to the egg? Why? The balance of pressure has changed. Fire needs oxygen to burn. As the fire burns, it uses up the oxygen inside the bottle and the force of the air pressure outside the bottle becomes greater than the pressure inside. The outside pressure pushes the egg into the bottle. Try different amounts of newspaper to see how little you need to suck in the egg.

Spaghetti Skyscraper

Supplies: *dry thick spaghetti, mini marshmallows, science journal and pencil, scissors, ruler, hard-boiled egg*

Design and construct a stable freestanding skyscraper. Will it be strong enough to support the weight of a hard-boiled egg?

1 Here's your challenge! Use spaghetti to construct your skyscraper's framework. The structure must support the egg's load. The base experiences the most stress, so figure out a way to make it extra strong. You can break the spaghetti into smaller pieces to build rectangular or square sections. With smaller pieces, build triangular supports. Use marshmallows for connectors.

2 What are some of the problems you can identify? Brainstorm some ideas and jot them down in your science journal.

3 Evaluate your building materials. Earlier in this book you tested spaghetti and marshmallows to determine if they are strong in tension or compression. Refresh your memory. Hold one piece of the brittle spaghetti between your index fingers. What happens when you push its opposite ends? How much force does it take for it to buckle or snap?

DID YOU KNOW?

The Empire State Building gets struck by lightning around 100 times each year! It was designed as a lightning rod for neighboring buildings.

4 Test the more flexible material. Place force on one marshmallow. Squash it with your finger. How does it hold up? What happens when you pull the sides? How much pulling distorts the shape?

5 Now that you understand your materials, start constructing some squares, rectangles, and triangles. Test to see if they handle compression or if they collapse. You should discover rectangles and squares break at the joints. That's where they are weakest. A triangle keeps its shape. It stays rigid and strong. What happens if you push spaghetti all the way through a marshmallow? Do the materials seem weaker or stronger? Can you make sure marshmallows firmly hold the spaghetti? How can you keep marshmallows from tearing or distorting?

6 Use your discoveries regarding the materials to sketch several possible skyscraper designs. How can triangles add structural support?

7 Follow your design as you start building. Remember, vertical sections of your skyscraper will be in compression. Horizontal and diagonal sections will probably be in tension. You may notice marshmallows at the base get distorted. That's where compression is concentrated. With distorted marshmallows, the skyscraper might collapse.

8 Select a place to carefully balance the hard-boiled egg. Does your structure support it?

TRY THIS

Use what you've learned about the strengths and weaknesses of your design. Try, try again! Make modifications and rebuild the structure.

AMAZING SKYSCRAPER ACHIEVEMENTS

ONCE YOU UNDERSTAND THE EXCEPTIONAL SKILL
of the engineers who ensure the safety of the world's skyscrapers
and the artistic talents of the architects who design them,
you'll forever marvel at these inspiring buildings. Modern
skyscrapers need to be eye-catching while also being able
to stand up to some of the world's most destructive forces.
From the tallest of the tall buildings to a modern pagoda
built to withstand tremors and typhoons to a steel giant rich
in cultural traditions, skyscrapers grace the world's skylines.

 88

AMAZING SKYSCRAPER ACHIEVEMENTS

CURRENT CHAMP: TALLEST OF THE TALL

- **Building and location:** Burj Khalifa, Dubai, United Arab Emirates, completed in 2010
- **Height:** 2,717 feet (828 meters)
- **Designed by:** Adrian Smith, American architect
- **Purposes:** residential, corporate offices, and hotel that includes an observation deck, park, fitness annex, and restaurants
- **Cost:** $1.5 billion

At the time of publication, Dubai's luxurious Burj Khalifa reigns as the world's tallest building. *Burj* is the Arabic word for "tower." That's appropriate, since this is the world's tallest freestanding tower and the world's tallest structure. The Burj Khalifa also boasts the world's highest swimming pool and fountain. One of the world's fastest elevators will zip you up to the world's highest observation deck on the 124th floor at over 26 miles per hour or 10 meters per second.

The Burj Khalifa is about twice as tall the Empire State Building. Yet somehow the structure looks deceptively delicate. Though constructed of steel, glass, and reinforced concrete, the skyscraper's design was actually influenced by a native desert flower called hymenocallis.

DID YOU KNOW?

London's dramatic 1,016-foot Shard is Europe's tallest skyscraper (310 meters). The triangular glass structure rises to a pointy top, designed to resemble slivers of glass.

The gleaming silver needle of the skyscraper stretches like the stem of the flower out of a **hexagonal** base. The three wings of the building spread like petals from the stem.

WORDS to KNOW

hexagonal: having six sides.

Windows bathe the building with sunlight and offer breathtaking views of the Persian Gulf. Unlike the skyscrapers of New York or Chicago, the Burj Khalifa rises like a lightning bolt in the sweltering desert, high above the rest of Dubai's skyline. This leaves the windows exposed to constant sun and summer temperatures that sizzle at 120 degrees Fahrenheit (49 degrees Celsius).

How does the Burj Khalifa beat the heat? Its 26,000 glass panels are designed to reflect the sun, providing a high level of sun protection.

Today, wind engineering is a critical aspect in the design of any new tall building, especially the very tallest of them all. Engineers conducted over 40 wind tunnel tests on Burj Khalifa to examine the effect wind would have on the tower and its occupants. To conquer the wind, the Burj Khalifa combines beauty and science in one tall package. Each branch of the building's Y-shaped design starts out thick at the base and gradually narrows around a central spire, making each wing a buttress for the other.

The nose of one branch of the Y faces into the prevailing direction of the wind, and breaks the force of the high-speed desert wind, sending it out and around the other two wings. If you've ever ridden close behind someone on a bike, you'll know that the person out front breaks the wind so the one behind can coast along without wind resistance.

DID YOU KNOW?

Even with its wind-breaking design, the 206-story Burj Khalifa will still sway slowly back and forth by about 6½ feet (2 meters) at the very top.

STEEL AND GLASS PAGODA: "STACKING UPWARD ON LUCK"

- **Building and location:** Taipei 101, Taipei, Taiwan, completed in 2004
- **Height:** 1,671 feet (509 meters)
- **Designed by:** C. Y. Lee and Partners, Taiwan
- **Purposes:** corporate offices, library, fitness center, shopping mall, observation deck
- **Cost:** $1.76 billion

Until the Burj Khalifa won the height race, China's Taipei 101 was the world's tallest building. Nonetheless, it was named the tallest and largest green building in the world in July 2011. Designed to withstand typhoons and tremors, the skyscraper is a magnificent steel-and-glass pagoda, a descendant of the earthquake-resistant Sai-in pagoda.

Architects designed the Taipei 101 Tower to look like a bamboo shoot, which symbolizes strength in Chinese culture.

The skyscraper's stunning design celebrates the Chinese lucky number 8, which is a symbol of success and prosperity. It connects present-day Taipei to its cultural heritage and inspires hope for the future. To stand up against earthquakes and typhoons, engineers constructed the skyscraper over 380 concrete piles, which were driven 262 feet into the ground (80 meters). Its eight sloped, symmetrical sections reduce ground-level winds.

To counter seismic movement when tremors rock the structure, the world's largest and heaviest tuned mass damper hangs like a giant pendulum visible inside the building from the 92nd floor down to the 88th floor. It swings up to five feet back and forth to reduce the sway of the building (1½ meters). Taipei 101 is considered one of the most stable buildings ever constructed.

SOARING TO THE FUTURE ON THE WINGS OF TRADITION

- **Building and location:** Petronas Twin Towers, Kuala Lumpur, Malaysia, completed in 1998
- **Height:** 1,483 feet (452 meters)
- **Designed by:** Argentina-born American architect César Pelli and Indonesian architect Achmad Murdija
- **Purpose:** the Petronas petroleum company's headquarters
- **Cost:** $1.6 billion

The world's tallest twin towers, Petronas Towers soar above Kuala Lumpur's high-tech district. The 88-story tapering skyscrapers are a striking combination of modern and traditional design. Its acres of steel shine in the daytime sunlight and are lit up spectacularly at night. The floor plan in the shape of two rotated squares forms an eight-pointed star that is traditional in Islamic art. This pattern continues all the way up the building, getting smaller as it rises. The marble floor design in each building's 40-story tower reflects a traditional weaving pattern.

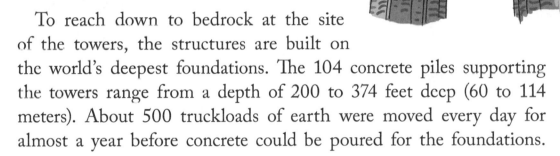

To reach down to bedrock at the site of the towers, the structures are built on the world's deepest foundations. The 104 concrete piles supporting the towers range from a depth of 200 to 374 feet deep (60 to 114 meters). About 500 truckloads of earth were moved every day for almost a year before concrete could be poured for the foundations.

THAT'S A LOT OF WINDOWS

Together, the towers have 55,000 glass panels. A reflective coating on the glass and mammoth steel visors protect people inside from the intense tropical sunlight. It takes window washers an entire month to wash each tower just once! Despite all that glass the French Spiderman still tried to climb the Petronas Towers with his bare hands and feet—twice! He reached the 60th floor both times before being arrested by the police.

The Skybridge connects the twin towers and represents the "gateway to the future." At 557 feet above the street (170 meters), it's the world's highest two-story bridge!

The Petronas Twin Towers are used mainly for office space, but they also contain a concert hall for the Malaysian Philharmonic Orchestra and two Muslim prayer rooms. The towers were the tallest buildings in the world from 1998 to 2004, until Taipei 101 reached higher. If you're in Kuala Lumpur, you won't need a map to find these towers—they're visible from almost anywhere in the city. From a distance, the towers resemble the letter M for Malaysia!

DID YOU KNOW?

The Royal Bank Plaza Towers' windows gleam in Toronto's sunlight. Each is coated with a glimmering layer of 24-karat gold! The windows, which contain $1 million in precious metal, provide a glitzy appearance. Since gold is a great insulator, they reduce heating bills, too.

AMAZING SKYSCRAPERS ACROSS THE GLOBE

Elephant Tower (Bangkok, Thailand, 1997)

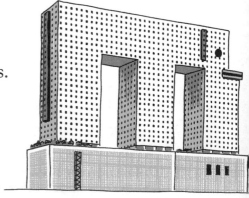

• Elephant Tower is 335 feet (102 meters) tall. It contains offices, condos, and shops.

This structure honors the importance of elephants in Thai culture and history.

- The urban complex is the world's largest elephant building. Three towers with dove-gray facades make up the body. Balconies form ears. Enormous round windows are eyes that watch over the city, while 20 stories of protruding rooms create a tail.

- Designed by architect Sumet Jumsai Na Ayudhaya, Elephant Tower even has tusks!

Shanghai World Financial Center (Shanghai, People's Republic of China, 2008)

- Shanghai World Financial Center is 1,614 feet (492 meters) high with offices, shops, and a hotel.

- The firm of Kohn Pedersen Fox designed the skyscraper with a dramatic shape. It links the heavens and Earth. Two sweeping arcs symbolize the heavens. A square prism represents Earth.

- This tallest building in the People's Republic of China has a light blue glass facade, and a very odd top. It looks like a bottle opener! A **trapezoidal** opening through the top is an ingeniously engineered design. Made of steel and reinforced concrete, it combats wind's load when it hits the skyscraper. Steel trusses support the structure. They hold up against seismic and wind forces with less steel than is typically used in other structures.

WORDS to KNOW

trapezoidal: shaped like a trapezoid, a four-sided figure with one pair of parallel sides.

Turning Torso (Malmo, Sweden, 2005)

- Turning Torso is a residential building rising 656 feet (200 meters), with 54 stories.

- Designed by Spanish architect and engineer Santiago Calatrava, Scandinavia's tallest skyscraper is unique because it is **asymmetrical**! Its design features a gigantic series of nine twisted cubes, each five stories high. The cubes are stacked one above the other at an angle, turning 90 degrees from bottom to top.

- Architect Calatrava is a sculptor who applies an artistic eye in creating structures. He's inspired by the human body's movements. Turning Torso is based on his marble sculpture of the same name. The elevators rise straight from the bottom to the top.

WORDS to KNOW

asymmetrical: not the same on both sides of a center line.

SKY HIGH FREEFALL

In 2012, Australian skydiver Felix Baumgartner leapt from 128,000 feet (39,014 meters), becoming the first human to break the speed of sound in freefall. Over 8 million people watched online, captivated by what many considered a risky publicity stunt. Wearing a specially engineered suit and helmet, Baumgartner rode a 334-foot-tall balloon (102 meters) into the stratosphere. Then the daredevil jumped!

With limited oxygen, Baumgartner plunged toward Earth. Would Baumgartner's suit malfunction? Would his blood boil? At **mach speed**, would his body tear apart like tissue paper?

WORDS to KNOW

mach speed: the speed of an object compared to the speed of sound.

Baumgartner accelerated rapidly, plummeting at 833.9 miles per hour (1,343 kilometers per hour), or mach 1.24. That's faster than the speed of sound. Baumgartner dove 24 miles through space (39 kilometers) before gliding safely to Earth.

How could he prepare for this stunt? By leaping over 2,500 times off vertical structures all over the world. He racked up six world records for BASE jumping, which is leaping from fixed objects using parachutes to break the fall. Twice Baumgartner set records for the highest BASE jump from a building, from a window-washing crane near the top of Petronas Towers and from Taipei 101.

**"We all have to fight our own fears,"
Baumgartner said. "We all have to set a
goal that's hard to accomplish."**

Toothpick Tower

Supplies: *flat toothpicks, glue, ruler, bucket, sand, scale, safety goggles*

When you build a freestanding toothpick tower, how much weight will it bear? Test your structure to find out!

1 What is the problem you are going to have to solve to build your tower? Brainstorm solutions and make predictions.

2 Build a simple, square 10-inch tower (25½ centimeters). Position the toothpicks as shown to construct each story. Glue the toothpicks in place. Continue building up until you reach the final height. Allow the glue to dry.

3 Fill the bucket halfway with sand. Weigh the filled bucket. Predict whether your tower will bear the weight.

4 Toothpicks could fly if the structure collapses, so wear goggles to test your prediction. Does the tower stand?

5 If your tower doesn't collapse, add more sand to the bucket. Test the structure with the heavier load.

TRY THIS

Construct the tower again. Modify the design. What can you do to help it bear more weight?

Weight Up, Gravity!

Supplies: *4 quarters, pencil, tracing paper, scissors, tape, ruler*

How will gravity, air resistance, and weight impact the speed at which two things fall?

1 Use your pencil to draw the outline of a quarter on the tracing paper. Cut out the paper coin. Make sure it's the same size as the actual quarter.

2 Hold the paper coin in one hand and the quarter in the other. They are the same size, but have different weights. What will happen when you drop them simultaneously?

3 Test your predictions. Release the quarters at the same time. What happens?

4 Conduct another test. Stack three quarters and tape them together. Place the fourth quarter at the edge of a table or counter. Position the stack of quarters at the edge, 2 inches away from the single coin (5 centimeters). Align the ruler behind the single coin and the stack of coins so that it is in contact with both.

5 Predict what will happen when you push the ruler against the coins and drop them from the edge. Test your predictions. What happens?

6 Do another test in the same way with two single quarters. What happens this time?

7 Draw conclusions. How does weight impact the speed at which an object falls?

TRY THIS

Test other pairs of items of different weights, such as a feather and book or a rock and a toothpick.

Starry Night Skyline

Supplies: *paper and pencil, ruler, file folders, scissors, glue, black construction paper, tissue paper, shiny gold wrapping paper*

Explore your own skyline or a famous skyline of the world. Create skyscrapers and other structures that portray a starlit cityscape.

1 Research iconic skylines for your own cityscape. What architectural features, such as spires and gargoyles make structures unique? Research the structures' heights.

2 Select five skyscrapers or structures to include. Prepare sample sketches of your skyline. How will you determine the structures' scale? How will you address height differences and building materials? What kinds of windows do your buildings have? Will you add a Ferris wheel or other unusual structure?

3 Refine your sketch, then cut your buildings out and trace the skyline onto the file folders to create a template. Cut out the template and glue it onto the black paper.

4 Be creative! Use tissue paper to add a nighttime glow to the windows. Use gold paper to accent the night sky.

5 Challenge a friend or family member to identify the completed skyline. Which structures did he or she recognize?

TRY THIS

Create an imaginary skyline that uses iconic skyscrapers from around the world—all in one place!

DISASTERS AND CLOSE CALLS

STANDING TALL OUTDOORS, VERTICAL STRUCTURES
are exposed to Mother Nature's strongest forces, including
storms and earthquakes. Skyscrapers face manmade
challenges too, such as aircraft collisions and fires. In addition
to the September 11, 2001, terrorist attacks, New York's
skyscrapers have endured several disasters and close calls.

B-52 BOMBER CRASHES INTO THE EMPIRE STATE BUILDING

It was a foggy morning in July 1945, during the final months of World War II, when the Empire State Building still soared as the world's tallest building. Suddenly, Manhattan residents were screaming and running for safety. Some feared they were under attack. Flying below 1,000 feet (305 meters), a US Army B-52 bomber roared down Fifth Avenue and crashed into the Empire State Building.

Captain William F. Smith was an experienced pilot who had been on a routine mission transporting servicemen to LaGuardia Airport. As the fog worsened, Smith radioed the airport and requested clearance to land. The air traffic controller warned Smith of zero-visibility conditions. He told Smith to remain in the air.

"Smith said, 'Thank you very much' and signed off," explains Arthur Weingarten, author of *The Sky Is Falling*, a book about the catastrophe. "He ignored it . . . He started to make a little bit of a turn that brought him over midtown Manhattan, and as he straightened out, the clouds broke up enough for him to realize he was flying among skyscrapers." The next thing he knew, he slammed into the north side of the Empire State Building.

Like an arrow, the bomber's tail protruded from the structure.

Smith and two crewmen died instantly. The violent impact hurled office workers across rooms, and wreckage tumbled to the streets. People were terrified the building would collapse.

In an instant, leaking gas ignited a fire that engulfed the 78th and 79th floors in flames. One man leaped from a window to escape the blaze but hundreds were trapped inside. Firefighters rescued most of them but, tragically, 11 office workers perished.

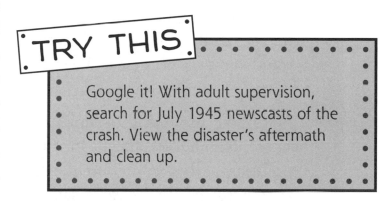

TRY THIS

Google it! With adult supervision, search for July 1945 newscasts of the crash. View the disaster's aftermath and clean up.

DID YOU KNOW?

At the exact moment of the B-52 Bomber's collision with the Empire State Building, an engineer with the Army Corps of Engineers was five blocks north of the skyscraper dictating a letter into a recording device. The recording captured the bomber's awful impact!

NEAR FATAL FLAW IN CITICORP CENTER

Building skyscrapers is a risky business. When an engineering failure occurs in an enormous structure, its impact is equally enormous.

The Citicorp Center's notorious close call could have been catastrophic.

Completed in 1977, the 59-story steel skyscraper is among New York's tallest buildings. Its roof slopes at a 45-degree angle, creating a unique appearance in Manhattan's skyline. For a time, the jumbo structure was dangerously fragile. From the start, the skyscraper presented a huge engineering puzzle. In the early 1970s, structural engineer William LeMessurier (1926–2007) planned the supporting skeleton. But St. Peter's Lutheran Church occupied a section of the proposed building site. A Gothic building with pointed arches, the church dated to 1905. The beloved church was in disrepair and would have to be demolished.

Citicorp purchased the property for $9 million, promising to build a new church at the site. Church officials insisted on several conditions. The new church would have to be constructed in the exact same location. No columns could be built through it. Connections to the new skyscraper were prohibited.

REBUILT CHURCH

CITICORP CENTER BUILDING

The design was a unique answer to an unusual problem.

LeMessurier faced an especially tall order. How did he rise to the challenge? He constructed the 915-foot skyscraper (279 meters) on four columns. These columns held up the tower on gigantic stilts. But LeMessurier didn't position the columns at the tower's corners. Instead, he placed them at the center of each side of the tower. One corner of the building cantilevered over the new church!

Notable Quotable

"Architecture is the language of a culture."
—*C. Y. Lee and Partners*

TRIBUTE IN LIGHT

After the terrorist attacks of September 11, the Municipal Art Society of New York engineered Tribute in Light. Beaming above Manhattan, Tribute in Light is visible over a 60-mile radius (97 kilometers). The society's website explains, "Tribute in Light was first presented on March 11, 2002, six months after the attacks, and MAS has presented it annually since. Comprising eighty-eight 7,000-watt xenon light bulbs positioned into two 48-foot squares that echo the shape and orientation of the Twin Towers, Tribute in Light is assembled each year on a roof near the World Trade Center site. The illuminated memorial reaches 4 miles into the sky and is the strongest shaft of light ever projected from earth into the night sky." The breathtaking work of art is a moving memorial to those who perished in the tragedy.

In 1978, after the Citicorp Center was occupied, an engineering professor questioned the design. He feared the building was flawed because of its column placement. He expressed doubts to his students. A student assigned to write about the skyscraper went straight to the top with his questions and called William LeMessurier. Insisting the structure was sound, LeMessurier explained that gigantic steel v-braces moved gravity and wind loads to the immense columns.

At first, LeMessurier considered the student a pest. But soon a huge concern nagged at the engineer.

LeMessurier discovered that the building's v-braces had been joined with bolted joints, which were cheaper than the far stronger welded joints. His findings frightened him. Bolted joints greatly reduced structural strength. Gusting diagonal winds could split the bolts. Joints would tear and the skyscraper would break apart and topple, launching disaster in the populous city.

Alarmed, LeMessurier hammered out a plan. To strengthen hundreds of bolted joints, workers would weld gigantic steel plates over them. LeMessurier rallied welders from as far away as Louisiana.

Working secretly through the night so they wouldn't ignite a panic, welders reinforced the skyscraper. With hurricane season approaching fast, the welders raced the clock for weeks. In the Atlantic Ocean, Hurricane Ella gained strength and took deadly aim at New York. Prepared for catastrophe, city officials held their breath. Weather services updated LeMessurier every three hours. The Red Cross stood by, armed with an emergency evacuation plan. Fortunately, Ella swerved and the storm headed off to sea.

Notable Quotable

"You're supposed to look beyond the interests of yourself and your client to society as a whole. And the most wonderful part of my story is that when I did it, nothing bad happened."
—*William LeMessurier*

We learn from close calls and failures as well as successes. The flawed structure remains a cautionary engineering tale.

LeMessurier's reinforcement efforts made the Citicorp Center one of the world's most structurally sound buildings!

DID YOU KNOW?

Close calls can happen anywhere. Boston's steel-and-glass John Hancock Tower is New England's tallest building. During construction and in high winds, double-layer glass windows started popping out. The sidewalk below was actually roped off to prevent pedestrians from getting hit by glass. This continued for three years! Empty windows were replaced with plywood, giving the building its nickname, the Plywood Palace. Eventually, the windows were replaced with single-layer glass, which solved the problem.

DESTRUCTION BY DESIGN

As an earsplitting blast rips the air, a towering skyscraper heaves and lurches and splits into sections. The pieces collide with a deafening clatter. The structure caves in like an enormous smashed aluminum soda can amid rolling clouds of ashy dust. Finally the building topples sideways in a mammoth mound of rubble. Gravity has done its job, with the help of a feat of engineering, **explosive demolition**.

WORDS to KNOW

explosive demolition: a planned, controlled process that takes down a structure with dynamite and other explosives.

Skyscrapers withstand forces to stand tall and resist collapse. But what happens when it's time to take down a vertical structure? How do engineers keep from wrecking neighboring buildings or hurting people with flying debris? How can a process called explosive demolition be highly controlled? First, blasters investigate the way the skyscraper's pieces are assembled. They walk through the skyscraper itself and assess support structures at every level.

WORDS to KNOW

detonate: to explode or cause to explode.

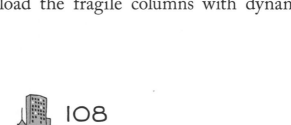

Then, armed with data, blasters determine which explosives will work best. They carefully load explosives at different levels in the skyscraper so that when blasters **detonate** explosives, the skyscraper will fall according to plan. It will cave in at different places, with sections collapsing against each another.

Next, workers get busy. They prepare for demolition. Crews knock down walls. They clobber support columns with sledgehammers to weaken them. Blasters load the fragile columns with dynamite or other explosives.

A MODERN MIRACLE

It's not just buildings that fail—scaffolding, the platforms supporting workers up high, does too! In 2007, brothers Edgar and Alcides Moreno were washing windows at an Upper East Side apartment building. Neither was wearing a safety harness when cables on their scaffolding suddenly snapped. Edgar plunged from the platform and died instantly. Meanwhile, Alcides plummeted 47 stories, clinging to his scaffolding platform. Scientists believe that the platform—and physics—saved his life.

The platform, 3 feet wide and 35 feet long (1 meter wide and 11 meters long), acted like a parachute to create enough wind resistance to slow the fall to about 45 miles per hour (72 kilometers per hour). Without it, Moreno would have hit the ground at a speed of over 100 miles per hour (161 kilometers per hour), according to Brian Schwartz, a professor of physics at the City University of New York.

WIND RESISTANCE

Miraculously, Alcides Moreno lived to tell his story. He broke 10 bones, but his head, pelvis, and spinal column were not damaged by the tremendous impact.

DID YOU KNOW?

In 2012, three brick workers in New York's Upper East Side endured a close call. While the men repaired a 21-story building's facade, one end of their scaffolding gave way and collapsed. Swaying from safety harnesses on the 17th floor, the men dangled precariously over the street. Minutes later, firefighters yanked them to safety through a window.

They clear the building and surrounding area for the safety of people and neighboring structures.

On demolition day, a siren wails. Brace for the big boom! The countdown begins. When the blaster presses the "fire" button, the skyscraper **implodes**. In just a few seconds, the building is destroyed. In an instant, the skyline changes.

WORDS to KNOW

implode: to collapse inward.

tsunami: a large, destructive wave caused by an earthquake.

DID YOU KNOW?

In 2011, a devastating 8.9 magnitude earthquake that hit Japan also triggered a **tsunami**. In *The New York Times*, Martin Fackler reported, "First came the roar and rumble of the temblor, shaking skyscrapers, toppling furniture and buckling highways. Then waves as high as 30 feet (9.14 meters) rushed onto shore, whisking away cars and carrying blazing buildings toward factories, fields and highways."

Nature's furies combined in deadly destruction and killed hundreds of people. Others scrambled to higher ground to escape a crushing wall of muddy water. People desperately clung to rooftops and bridges, stranded without food and water. The quake pulverized older buildings into instant rubble. Vertical and horizontal shaking slammed newer skyscrapers, which swayed like reeds in the wind. Would they topple? Earthquake resistant, they remained upright. But Japan's killer quake bent the tip of the 1,092-foot (333-meter) Tokyo Tower.

Notable Quotable

"Learn from yesterday, live for today, hope for tomorrow.
The important thing is not to stop questioning."
—*Albert Einstein*

Shake It Up!

Supplies: *shoebox with lid, scissors, marbles, stapler, 4 rubber bands, sugar cubes, glue*

Shake tables test the impact of earthquakes on structures, helping scientists assess the abilities of different structures in resisting seismic shaking. Can you construct a tower that will hold up under vertical and horizontal motion at your own shake table?

1 Place the shoebox on a sturdy surface. Cut off the lid's rectangular section. Trim that piece to fit inside the box with a 1-inch clearance on all sides (2½ centimeters). There should be enough space inside the box so the lid section moves both vertically and horizontally.

2 Place a layer of marbles inside the box. Staple one rubber band to each corner of the box. Carefully stretch the opposite, unstapled part of each band and staple each in turn to the lid section.

3 To test the shake table, tug the lid section toward one side of the box. Release it. The marbles should set it in motion.

4 Construct a tower with sugar cubes and glue. Allow the glue to dry completely. Predict how your tower will hold up to shaking. Test your predictions.

5 Test different building materials. What other materials can you use to build more structures? Do they survive the shake table?

111

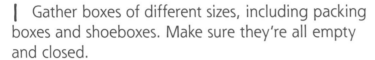

BUILD IT YOURSELF

Stack It Skyscraper

Supplies: *cardboard boxes of different sizes, paper and pencil, glue, duct tape, paper towel tube, toys for gargoyles, natural elements such as sticks and grass for hawk's nest, craft knife, markers*

Use cardboard boxes of different sizes to build a skyscraper. Design a spire and add windows, gargoyles, a hawk's nest, and other features.

1 Gather boxes of different sizes, including packing boxes and shoeboxes. Make sure they're all empty and closed.

2 Assess the weight of each box and think about their strength and stability. Separate the boxes according to weight and size. Build vertically with boxes of gradually decreasing weight and size.

3 Sketch a design for a skyscraper with a spire. Consider your assessment of the boxes' weights. Include areas to decorate the skyscraper with gargoyles. Plan a secure ledge for a hawk's nest.

4 Choose the box with the greatest heft to use as your structure's base. Place it on the floor.

5 Build up following your design. Use trial and error to find the best building methods. Glue the second box to the first. Reinforce it with duct tape. Continue your vertical construction until you use the final box.

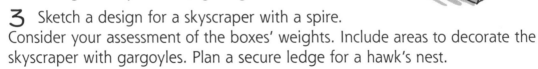

DID YOU KNOW?

Most skyscraper disasters involve fires. In 2012, flames devoured Moscow's Federation Tower, which was still under construction. When complete, the skyscraper will take the title as Europe's tallest building.

6 Glue the tube in place to form a spire. Glue the gargoyles in place and build the hawk's nest on its ledge.

7 Draw some windows on the skyscraper. Ask an adult to help you use the craft knife to cut the cardboard away to reveal the windows. Decorate your building, using your imagination and creativity.

TRY THIS

Assess your structure. Did it remain stable on the base? Is it straight, or does it lean? Do you notice design flaws? How would you make modifications?

FARMSCRAPER

Singapore's Jack Ng grows bok choy and cabbages indoors in his A Gro-Go "farmscraper." Using trays stacked in aluminum towers reaching 30 feet high (9 meters), Ng says his farmscraper grows over five times the vegetables produced in traditional farming. He grows plants close to grocery stores so his vertical farm cuts down on transportation costs and reduces carbon emissions. On the island of Singapore and other areas where land is scarce, vertical farming could be a trend on the rise.

Index Card Tower

Supplies: *28 index cards—3 inches by 5 inches (7.6 by 12.7 centimeters),
10 inches clear tape (25 centimeters), paper and pencil,
ruler, scissors, stopwatch, stuffed animal*

**Use creativity and engineering skills to design and construct
a stable, balanced index card tower. Here's your challenge.
Your tower must support a stuffed animal at a height of
at least 12 inches (30½ centimeters). At its top, it must
bear the animal's weight for at least 15 seconds.**

1 Use index cards and tape as building materials. Use
the ruler and scissors as tools only. They can't form part
of the structure. You can bend, cut, fold, and roll cards.
Use engineering skills to form beams and girders. How
can you construct a sturdy foundation for the tower?
How can you create triangular sections to
build braces and frames? How can you
connect and reinforce sections? Let
your ideas fly!

2 Evaluate your building
materials. Use three index
cards and 4 inches of
tape (10 centimeters) as
test materials. Push, pull,
and twist them. How do they hold up
to tension and compression? To torsion?

3 Experiment with building. Construct some tubes, squares, triangles, and
other shapes. Test to see if they handle forces. Evaluate the strengths and
weaknesses of each shape.

4 Using your discoveries about the building materials and different shapes, sketch several possible tower designs. Choose your best design and start building!

5 Once your tower is complete, get the stopwatch ready. Carefully place the stuffed animal at the top. Does the tower hold its weight for 15 seconds? Does the structure stay balanced?

6 Evaluate your design. How can you modify the tower for added strength and stability?

TRY THIS

Extend the challenge! Test to find out if your tower can support the weights of other objects. Watch what happens to your tower as you test light objects and heavy ones.

ELEVATOR DROP

In 1945 at the age of 19, Betty Lou Oliver was an elevator operator in the Empire State Building. When an airplane crashed into the building, its engines flew off. One engine sliced through some elevator cables and two elevators plummeted into the sub-basement. Oliver broke her back, neck, and pelvis in the crash. Today, her 1,000-foot plunge down 75 stories is an entry in the Guinness Book of World Records (304 meters). She survived the longest elevator shaft fall!

You're the Engineer and the Architect!

Supplies: *aluminum foil, blocks, cardboard boxes, clamps, craft sticks, dowel rods, duct tape, emery board, foam egg cartons, glue, masking tape, modeling clay, paper clips, pencil, paper towel or toilet paper tubes, plastic milk jugs, PVC tubing, scissors, straws, string or twine, toothpicks*

Through innovation, engineers solve problems. Use the engineering design process to create a tall structure that solves a problem. Base the problem on one in your community, such as limited space or earthquake vulnerability.

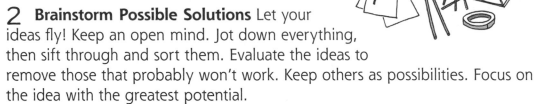

1 **Identify the Problem** What do you need to accomplish? Ask questions. Gather information and set your goal.

2 **Brainstorm Possible Solutions** Let your ideas fly! Keep an open mind. Jot down everything, then sift through and sort them. Evaluate the ideas to remove those that probably won't work. Keep others as possibilities. Focus on the idea with the greatest potential.

3 **Design and Draw a Plan** Draw a diagram and plan for your solution. Choose tools and building materials you'll need. Add your own items, too.

4 **Build the Prototype** Use tools and materials to make a mock-up. Notice anything that seems like it won't work.

5 **Test the Prototype** Conduct tests to see if it's sturdy. Give it a push or a pull. Does it withstand forces and loads? Will it resist collapse?

6 **Evaluate Success** What worked well or didn't work with the design? What adjustments will improve your structure? What other materials can you use?

7 **Redesign with Improvements** Try, try again!

acceleration: moving faster, increasing in speed.

ancient Mesopotamia: an area in what is today southern Iraq.

archaeologist: someone who studies ancient cultures by looking at what they left behind.

architect: a person who designs buildings.

asymmetrical: not the same on both sides of a center line.

BCE: put after a date, BCE stands for Before Common Era and counts down to zero. CE stands for Common Era and counts up from zero. These non-religious terms correspond to BC and AD.

bedrock: the layer of solid rock deep underground, under the top layer of soil and loose rock.

bionic: a body part involving electronics.

brace: to support or strengthen.

buckling: the sudden crumbling or falling down that occurs when the force of compression overcomes an object's capacity to handle that compression.

buttress: a support that adds stability to a wall or building.

cantilevered: a projected structure attached or supported only on one end.

cargo: a load of something.

center of gravity: the point in an object at which gravity is concentrated.

cityscape: a view of a city.

civil engineering: the branch of engineering that deals with the design, construction, and maintenance of public works and public buildings or spaces.

civilization: a community of people that is advanced in art, science, and government.

collapse: to fall in or down suddenly.

column: a vertical support structure.

compression: a pushing force that squeezes or presses a material inward.

convection: the massive vertical movement of heat or fire.

counterweights: equal weights that cause an object to be balanced.

culture: a group of people who share beliefs and a way of life.

curtain walls: the outside skin of a skyscraper, often made of windows.

dead load: the actual, constant weight of a structure.

detonate: to explode or cause to explode.

dynamic load: load that changes over time and is applied through motion.

energy: the ability to do work.

engineering: the work done by engineers.

engineer: someone who uses science, math, and creativity to solve problems.

entasis: a bulge in a column's shaft, which creates a slight curvature.

equilibrium: the state of balance between opposing forces.

erosion: the gradual wearing away of rock and soil by water and wind.

excavate: to dig out material from the ground.

explosive demolition: a planned, controlled process that takes down a structure with dynamite and other explosives.

GLOSSARY

facade: the outside or front of a building.

filament: the wire thread in an electric bulb that glows when heated by a current.

footing: an embedded anchor for columns in a foundation.

force: a push or pull that changes an object's motion.

foundation: the part of a building below the ground that transfers and distributes the structure's weight.

fulcrum: the point on which a lever turns or pivots.

gargoyle: an architectural element that serves as a rainspout, often in the form of distorted humans and animals.

geometric: straight lines and simple shapes such as circles or squares.

girder: a strong horizontal supporting beam, usually made of steel.

gravity: a physical force that draws everything toward the center of the earth.

hexagonal: having six sides.

implode: to collapse inward.

incandescent: containing a wire that glows when heated by an electric current.

inertia: the tendency of a body at rest to remain at rest or a body in motion to stay in motion—until a force acts on it.

innovate: to come up with a new way of doing something.

landmark: an important structure or feature of the land that identifies a place and can be used to find or mark a location.

lever: a simple machine made of a rigid bar that pivots on a support, called a fulcrum.

live load: the changing weight of vehicles, people, furniture, and other things that are placed on a structure.

load: an applied force or weight.

mach speed: the speed of an object compared to the speed of sound.

matter: what an object is made of.

medieval: the period of time in European history from about 350 CE to about 1450 CE. Also called the Middle Ages.

metropolis: a very large and important city.

neural: related to a nerve or the central nervous system.

open-ended: able to adapt to the needs of a situation.

optical illusion: a trick of the eyes that makes people see something differently than it really is.

ornate: elaborately decorated.

panoramic: a wide, unobstructed view in all directions.

patent: having the exclusive right to make, use, or sell something.

patrician: a member of one of ancient Rome's wealthiest families.

pendulum: a weight hung from a fixed support so it swings by gravity.

physics: the science of how matter and energy work together.

pilgrim: a traveler on a journey to a holy place.

prosthesis: an artificial body part.

prototype: a working model or mock-up that allows engineers to test their solution.

public work: a construction project such as a highway or dam that is paid for by the government for use by anyone.

ravage: to cause severe damage to something.

rebar: a reinforced steel bar that is added to concrete to make a stronger building material.

replica: an exact copy of something.

scaffolding: a temporary wooden platform used to support construction workers.

seismic: the earth's vibrations and tremors during an earthquake.

settlement load: a change in soil as a mammoth structure settles into the ground.

shear: a sliding force that slips parts of a material in opposite directions.

skeleton frame: a skyscraper's support structure.

skyline: an outline of land and buildings against the sky.

skyscraper: an extremely tall building.

snapping: the splitting apart that occurs when the force of tension overcomes an object's ability to handle that tension.

stable: steady and firm, not changing.

statics: how forces work together to keep objects in balance.

structurally sound: stable and able to resist collapse.

structure: something that is built, such as a building, bridge, tunnel, tower, or dam.

substructure: the underground area of a skyscraper that supports the structure.

superstructure: the area of a skyscraper above the foundation.

sustainable: able to continue with little effect on the environment.

technology: tools, methods, and systems used to solve a problem or do work.

tension: a pulling force that pulls or stretches a material outward.

thrust: a reactive pressure or force.

torsion: a twisting force that turns or twirls a material.

trapezoidal: shaped like a trapezoid, a four-sided figure with one pair of parallel sides.

tremor: a shaking movement or small earthquake.

trial and error: trying first one thing, then another and another, until something works.

truss: a network of beams and bars that rely on triangles to support a load.

tsunami: a large, destructive wave caused by an earthquake.

tycoon: a wealthy, powerful person in business or industry.

vaulted: a building or room with an arched roof or roofs.

waterscape: a landscape with an expanse of water as a dominant feature.

wind load: the force of moving air on a structure.

ziggurat: an ancient pyramid-shaped temple tower.

BOOKS

Caney, Steven. *Steven Caney's Ultimate Building Book*, Running Press Kids, 2006.

Glancey, Steven. *The Story of Architecture*. Dorling Kindersley, 2000.

Latham, Donna. *Bridges and Tunnels: Investigate Feats of Engineering*. Nomad Press, 2012.

Latham, Donna. *Canals and Dams: Investigate Feats of Engineering*. Nomad Press, 2013.

Macaulay, David. *Building Big*. Houghton Mifflin, 2000.

Salvadori, Mario. *The Art of Construction: Projects and Principles for Beginning Engineers & Architects*. Chicago Review Press, 2000.

Sullivan, George. *Built to Last: Building America's Amazing Bridges, Dams, Tunnels, and Skyscrapers*. Scholastic, 2005.

Yee. *Origami Architecture: Papercraft Models of the World's Most Famous Buildings*. Tuttle, 2011.

WEB SITES

Council on Tall Buildings and Urban Habitats: The Skyscraper Center
www.skyscrapercenter.com/

EngineerGirl!
www.engineergirl.org/

Discovery Channel: Extreme Engineering
dsc.discovery.com/convergence/engineering/engineering.html

Latest Earthquakes in the World
earthquake.usgs.gov/earthquakes/recenteqsww/

Museum of Science: Structures and Forces
www.mos.org/etf/force.html

PBS: Building Big
www.pbs.org/wgbh/buildingbig/

Skyscraper Museum
www.skyscraper.org/home.htm

Society of Women Engineers: Educational Outreach
aspire.swe.org/

UNESCO World Heritage List
whc.unesco.org/en/list

Women at Work Museum
www.womenatworkmuseum.org/envision-engineering.html